This Is Bass Lake

This Is Bass Lake: A Destination for Generations was produced in partnership with the Bass Lake Property Owners Association, a not-for-profit all-volunteer organization committed to promoting the physical and social welfare of its members and to maintaining and protecting their property and other general interests. Through the support of its nearly three hundred members, the BLPOA offers residents around the lake a way to connect, communicate, and come together for the common purpose of supporting the health and well-being of the lake.

Bass Lake Property Owners Association
PO Box 1052
Pentwater, MI 49449

Mission Point Press

Mission Point Press

Published by Mission Point Press
MissionPointPress.com

Cover art by Neva Chapman
Cover Design: Deirdre Wait
Interior Design: Eddie Vincent

Library of Congress: 2025905150

ISBN: 978-1-965278-95-6

Printed in the United States of America

About the cover:
In the early 1930s, Neva Gilbert Chapman captured on canvas a quintessential memory of her son, Ted, as he stepped out on their dock to go fishing on a brilliant Bass Lake day. The boy was quite annoyed at the time about having to stand and pose as his mother sketched this scene because it was taking away from his fishing time.

Praise for *This Is Bass Lake: A Destination for Generations*

"With meticulous research and vivid storytelling, the Bass Lake History Committee brings the history of Bass Lake to life, capturing the spirit of its people, the richness of its landscapes, and the echoes of its past. As someone who grew up here, I found this book both deeply familiar and surprisingly relevant — uncovering forgotten stories, illuminating well-known legends, and weaving them together in a way that makes history feel alive. A must-read for anyone who loves Bass Lake or simply appreciates masterful historical storytelling."

Dick Warner
President, Pentwater Historical Society

"*This Is Bass Lake: A Destination for Generations* is a tapestry of the 110-year history of a beloved vacation destination that has drawn generations of visitors to its shores. Compiled from both personal stories and the broader historical context of the region, this collection explores the area's rich past — from its early settlers and indigenous roots to the rise of bustling resorts and charming cottages. Brimming with cherished memories, folklore, and historical accounts, it paints a vivid picture of a lakeside retreat that became a summer haven for so many. Organized for easy reading, this book offers a journey through time, celebrating the spirit of a community that continues to thrive."

Amy Vander Zwart
Editor, *Pentwater Pride*

"As a relative newcomer to Bass Lake (circa 1975), a historic flat tire forever linked my family to Whispering Surf Campground and Bass Lake. *This Is Bass Lake: A Destination for Generations* has eloquently captured the rich history of this remarkable western Michigan 'hidden gem.' The Bass Lake History Committee's dedication and commitment to this project has resulted in the delivery of a comprehensive look into Bass Lake's storied past, including an in-depth review of the all-volunteer lake association founded in 1915. Through responsible stewardship, the Bass Lake Property Owners Association continues more than a century of service to Bass Lake residents and safeguards the lake's natural beauty and tranquil landscape for generations to come."

Dan James
President, Bass Lake Property Owners Association

This Is Bass Lake

A Destination for Generations

As told by the
Bass Lake History Committee

How To Get There!

Dedication

To those family members and friends who came before us and introduced us to Bass Lake so that we, too, may know the joy of the Bass Lake experience.

Contents

PART 2

Preface

Over a hundred years ago, a few people, primarily from the greater Chicago area, discovered a tranquil summer oasis near an enchanting lake with a meandering outlet that flowed out to Lake Michigan. When these intrepid pioneers arrived at Bass Lake near Pentwater, Michigan, they had no way of knowing that their beloved haven would become a legacy for future generations who would cherish the lake just as much as these early settlers did. For those who have known and loved Bass Lake for all of their lives, the magnetic pull to return year after year is strong, and summer isn't complete until one has experienced the familiar sights, sounds, and smells and gotten that Lake Michigan sand between his or her toes at the Bass Lake Outlet.

Mary Lambrix (also referred to as Mrs. Roscoe Lambrix) was president of the Bass Lake Park Improvement Association in 1954. Based on the dates on letters and narratives from 1955, indications are that Mrs. Lambrix attempted to document the history of Bass Lake by asking some of the old-timers to write personal accounts of their own Bass Lake stories. The authors of these original accounts are names you'll recognize, because you will still see them on cottage signs and mailboxes around the lake: Chapman, Finch, Wanzer, Gilbert, Thiele, Hillman, and Ramsey.

Some of these documents made their way into a scrapbook, others were passed down within the author's own family or the Bass Lake Property Owners Association, and a few more were filed with local historical societies. We're grateful for those long gone who wrote down their memories so that we may share in their recollections of the early years and understand why Bass Lake was so special to them.

The members of the Bass Lake History Committee had grandparents,

parents, and other family members who shared stories and personal accounts of their early days at Bass Lake. We realized that as we were losing these loved ones, we didn't want to lose their stories about the early days and their connections to Bass Lake. Our desire was to be able to document these fascinating and memorable stories in order to share them with future generations who will also love our lake.

This book began with a scrapbook—a treasure trove of historical documents, poems, photographs, newspaper clippings, letters, invitations, and much more—collected over the past century. When the scrapbook was presented to introduce the history project at a Bass Lake Property Owners Association meeting in 2021, a team of volunteers eagerly signed on to use it as the inspiration to create a true, documented history of Bass Lake, and they have spent countless hours weaving these memories together for you to enjoy and understand why we keep returning to this place we love. We thank the Bass Lake Property Owners Association for recognizing the value in compiling these early personal accounts and more recent happenings at Bass Lake.

Over the next three years, dozens of Bass Lake families contributed to the project—sharing photos, family histories, memoirs, transcripts from interviews, and personal stories. Just so you know … almost everything in this book is true. Many of these experiences and stories are shared by multiple families, and they each have their own version of the truth. Wherever possible, we have endeavored to accurately report events and to faithfully represent the intent of individual contributors. As Harry Hillman III so aptly observed in his telling of his family's Bass Lake history, "I am sure that my version will be different from what other people may write, as we all remember things differently, and things are seen by different families from different viewpoints. Please remember in reading this that the history told by one old-timer is not more correct or incorrect than that told by another." We sincerely apologize for any content in this book that is not completely accurate or was not properly acknowledged.

The contributors to these stories span all ages and six generations. Overwhelmingly, from this vast range of voices, two central themes emerge. The first is the sublime beauty of Bass Lake and its surroundings—the familiar nature of Bass Lake, a mystical place where time stands still, year after year, decade after decade. The other, more importantly, is connection with friends and family and the traditions consisting of the same simple pleasures enjoyed by previous generations at Bass Lake. The feeling we have while we're at Bass Lake is renewable each year, revives us in the colder months, and leaves us with the longing to return next summer.

We sincerely hope you will enjoy reading this book as much as we did compiling it. Perhaps these stories will spark familiar memories, make you chuckle, and endear Bass Lake to you even more, now that you know the rest of the story.

Bass Lake History Committee 2021–25
Barbara Barrow Achenbaum, Carla Barrow, Kyle and Pam Chapman,
Wendy Wanzer Jonkers, and Charity Gilbert Monroe

Introduction

Ted Chapman grew up spending his summers at Bass Lake, and the love he had for the lake and the family cottage lasted not only for his lifetime but carried on to future generations. Being at the lake each summer was so ingrained into the fabric of his being that, as a college student in Indiana, he would hitchhike to Bass Lake just for the weekend in order to spend a few more precious hours at the lake. As many Bass Lakers do, Ted grew up, got married, and brought his own family every summer to enjoy Bass Lake. He was also devoted to the Bass Lake Park Improvement Association and served as its president from 1956–1957. In his spring newsletter that year, knowing his readers would be eagerly anticipating their summer return to the lake, Ted shared the essence of Bass Lake in the following excerpt:

The gentle slap of the waves against the side of a boat—the rolling hills to the North, dotted with orchards and fields of grain—the infinite patience of the long-stemmed heron, a paragon among fishermen—the moon, a silver path dancing its way across the lake only to disappear in the darkness of the distant shore—a storm, whitecaps scudding before the wind, and the supple forest trees bending almost to the ground— aftermath, a brilliant sky and only the sound of distant rollers pounding the beach to serve as a reminder of nature's fury—a turtle, startled from his siesta by the splash of an oar, scoots from his log and disappears silently among the lily pads— the putt-putt of a late evening fisherman returning home, sometimes empty-handed, but never too discouraged, to try again—a chipmunk, darting along the fence and pausing to peer intently at the two-legged creatures who invade his kingdom every summer—children splashing in the Outlet and searching for pirate gold in the dune grasses above—a gaunt pine, clinging valiantly to the side of a dune, its life dependent upon the vagaries of the shifting sand—a swimmer, cautiously feeling his way out to the second sandbar—a beach supper, hot dogs, marshmallows, and who cares about the sand—the indescribable beauty of a Lake Michigan sunset—the Outlet, funneling under the bridge and then twisting and weaving its way lazily around the base of Eagle Top until finally, with a westerly turn, it flows past the home of the fairies, tumbles over the dam, and scampers across the beach to the welcoming arms of the Big Lake—the Little Lake, a mirror in that moment of repose. All this is Bass Lake.

PART 1

Watching the sunrise over Bass Lake from the Outlet bridge. This is the essence of a Bass Lake morning.

Chapter 1
Bass Lake Discovered

This Is a Bass Lake Morning

THIS is a Bass Lake Morning
The wind is in the Pines!
Wavelets are dancing, and the golden sun shines.
The shimmering Outlet beckons, Lily pads gleam—
At the end of the passage is a wide blue dream!
Roses and herons and shadowed ponds …
Are there for the finding mid several shades of green.
A turtle is the captain of a log near the pier—
See a Bass Lake morning, and you'll have it for all your years.

—Jean Gilbert Kraybill

Bass Lake, near Pentwater, Michigan, has been a delightful summer refuge for generations of those seeking a cool, quiet escape on its shores. Long before the days of family picnics and leisurely paddles around the lake, Bass Lake was a settling place for Native Americans and played an important role in the logging industry. The denuded forests were fertile hunting grounds for individuals and hunting clubs from the Chicago area, as well as a retreat for church members. Bass Lake's glistening shores beckoned local Pentwater residents and eventually others who traveled great distances to revel in its natural beauty.

Charles Mears was just a boy when he and his brothers studied John Farmer's *Map of Michigan*. Mears was born in 1814 outside Boston, where his father owned the locks on the Middlesex Canal. Mears and his brothers learned firsthand the lumber trade, as well as the control of water power for dams and mill machinery. In 1835, the Mears brothers looked to the West for new adventures. Believing the promises of that never forgotten brochure promoting emigration to the state—where lumber was abundant and the fledgling industry looked promising—the brothers headed to Michigan.

In 1838, the Mears brothers scouted a number of areas for potential lumber mills along the west Lake Michigan shoreline. They settled initially in an area now known as Whitehall and were the first white settlers in the area. Over the next twenty-five years, Charles Mears purchased about forty thousand acres of land in Michigan, including the land surrounding Bass Lake. He constructed and operated fifteen mills and built six harbors along Michigan's western coast to transport his lumber. Pentwater became a bustling village.

From 1840 until the turn of the 19th century, most of Michigan's forests were cut down to create farms and to supply lumber for buildings, ships, and mines. Michigan was the nation's leading lumber producer—primarily white pines—between 1870 and 1900.

In the late 19th century, entrepreneurs in the lumber business were drawn to the vast amount of pine trees around Bass Lake. One of those was Martin S. Perkins, a Civil War veteran and native of New York state. Having previously owned a mill in Coldwater, Michigan, before the war, Perkins moved to Pentwater after the war. He opened a steam-driven sawmill at the Bass Lake Outlet, which he enlarged and dammed for his logging business. A primitive bridge, in the same place the current bridge is today, was used to transport the cut slabs to town. An industrious man, Perkins also ran a thriving Pentwater bus-and-transfer service. His horse, Doc, pulled a wagon that met the ferry and transported passengers and freight.

Pine lumber was in great demand after the Chicago Fire of 1871, and the harvesting of western Michigan pine exploded. At this time, the raker tooth saw had been invented, which increased logging efficiency and production. Loggers were interested only in harvesting and dumped whatever they didn't need, having little regard for how the surrounding area was left. The woods surrounding Bass Lake had been clear-cut, and the land stripped of first-growth pine, with only scrub trees, unwanted debris, and old logging trails remaining.

Bass Lake Recreation Park

In 1886, two decades after Pentwater was settled, a group of residents seeking a new destination for recreation became intrigued by the much smaller lake situated four miles north of Pentwater. Although the Bass Lake landscape had changed dramatically after the lumber industry boom, many new trees had been planted around the lake—and it was only a half-hour drive over an uneven dirt road through wild and attractive scenery. Bass Lake, less than a mile from Lake Michigan, was also accessible by boat. Visitors soon discovered that Bass Lake was a pleasant spot for a day's outing of fishing and picnicking, and they began to coalesce around the idea of making significant improvements for the public to enjoy.

Development of Bass Lake officially began when three prominent Pentwater residents decided that it would be feasible to establish a resort there. These men were William Ambler, an attorney and former state senator; Dr. George Cleveland, a physician; and Martin Perkins. They approached Charles Mears, and the Pentwater group found Mr. Mears to be favorable toward the project. Mears suggested the formation of a company to which he would convey the land for seventy-five dollars. He was the first official stockholder of Bass Lake property, and others followed suit in this investment.

Such a generous offer could hardly be passed up, and articles of incorporation were promptly drawn up. The shares were set at twenty-five dollars each. Within the week, six hundred dollars more in stock was purchased. It was decided quickly to make the road passable, to take the underbrush out of the grove, and to build a boathouse pavilion. A year later, the grounds were completed for the newly created Bass Lake Recreation Park.

Once the pavilion was completed, several buildings followed, including a kitchen, a boathouse and dock, two bathhouses, and an icehouse. Two clay croquet courts and swings were installed. A swimming beach was cleared, and sightseeing boats were available at fifteen cents per hour. The pavilion was equipped with tables and rustic rockers, and benches were scattered about the grounds. Because of the popularity of the Recreation Park, which saw a daily stream of visitors, it was deemed advisable by the membership to set up some rules and hire a caretaker to see that they were enforced.

On the western shore of Bass Lake, about halfway between the Bass Lake Recreation Park and the channel to the Outlet, a small enclave of cottages known as Boody's Landing existed in the 1880s. At that time, Pentwater was a lumber town, and some of the more prominent citizens had perhaps ten cottages at Bass Lake. In the early 1890s, the cottages caught fire, and all burned. In the early 1900s, ashes and burned trees were the only evidence of the former resort.

Hymns, Honeymoons, and Hunters

About this time, some members of the First Baptist Church of Austin, Illinois, discovered Bass Lake as a place to connect with nature and worship together. These church members held frequent religious services and often rowed their boats into the center of the lake and sang hymns in the evening twilight. They bathed in Lake Michigan at the Outlet. The understanding was that if one could get the family up to this place, it should be possible to spend the summer at a very low cost in these bucolic surroundings.

Bertha P. Finch was a widowed schoolteacher and member of the church. At the turn of the century, Chicago schoolteachers were paid on a ten-month basis, so Bertha viewed spending the summer months at Bass Lake with her two children to be a prudent financial decision, as well as an opportunity for fellowship with other friends from their church. George B. Finch, Bertha's son, came to Bass Lake for the first time in 1903 as a young boy of six. By the time young George spent his first summer at Bass Lake, the logged-off land around Bass Lake had been replanted with pine, and red oak saplings were starting to grow. "I'm as tall as the trees!" exclaimed the delighted lad. George loved being at Bass Lake so much that he honeymooned with his new bride there in 1921 and returned each summer for the rest of his life.

Neva Julia Gilbert was a young girl of fourteen in 1893 when her father, who was in the real estate business, traded a pocket watch for land near Pentwater. After traveling overnight by boat across Lake Michigan on the

SS *Mabel Bradshaw*, named for the owner's wife and operated by Captain Perkins, Wallace Gilbert and his family arrived at the dock in the fishing village of Pentwater. Upon inspection, the newly acquired land was found to be nothing but empty dunes below the town, and it proved to be a big disappointment. Nevertheless, the Gilberts made the best of it, rented a tent and boat, and enjoyed a relaxing week fishing and camping on the newly acquired beach property.

On Sunday morning, the Gilberts rowed across the harbor and visited the Baptist Church in Pentwater. After a cordial visit with the minister, they enthusiastically accepted an invitation to join his family on a camping trip

Chapman family

Neva Gilbert was happy to be at Bass Lake, even though her family was roughing it and sleeping in a tent circa 1900.

to a little nearby lake called Bass Lake. The men left by boat a day ahead of the women, camped on the beach overnight, and entered the outlet stream to Bass Lake the following morning. The women followed with a horse team and wagon loaded down with tents, supplies, and groceries, and the two parties met at the camping spot on the west shore of Bass Lake, south of the Outlet, where the Dr. Newell Gilbert Cottage now stands.

The following summer, the Gilbert family eagerly returned to the same location to camp at Bass Lake for six weeks. In the woods, two tents were properly set up with slanting ground and trenches at the side to carry any rain downhill and away from the tent. One tent was used for food supplies and cooking, while the other housed beds covered with high net canopies.

The Dr. Gilbert Cottage is located where the road makes the first sharp curve to the west when headed north on Lakeshore Drive from the Wishing Well. Dr. Robert Gilbert was the son of Dr. Clark Gilbert and the grandson of Newell Gilbert. The Newell Gilberts and Wallace Gilberts were close friends but not related, and neither of these Gilbert families were related to John Gilbert, who married into the Finch family.

That summer, no one else lived on the whole west side of Bass Lake, except for one old hermit and his dog, but the Gilberts became friendly with the families across the lake.

In 1896, Wallace B. Gilbert, with his partner, Frank Pray, bought what was to be surveyed and laid out as Gilbert's Addition to Bass Lake Park, a parcel of about sixty acres running along the northwest shore of Bass Lake, south to where Bass Lake Boulevard turns west back toward Lakeshore Drive. Mr. Gilbert did not have the resources to plot his land into a saleable subdivision, so he sought help from Mr. Frank Race, who was in the real estate business in Austin, Illinois. Mr. Race's daughter, Myrtle, later married a man named Lattin, for whom Lattin Road is named. Also in the real estate business at this time in Austin and Oak Park were Henry F. Thiele Sr. and Harry F. Hillman Sr. Enthusiasm for Bass Lake spread in the Austin/Oak Park area, and many of the original families who came to the area and purchased property were connected through friendships or relationships with the previously mentioned real estate groups, churches, or families. The first Hillman family property at Bass Lake was acquired in lieu of some sort of real estate commission, which stands to reason since very little cash had changed hands since the trading of the Wallace Gilbert pocket watch.

Neva Gilbert met Edgar K. Chapman while they were both teaching at DeKalb (Illinois) High School. They were married in 1907 and honeymooned at Bass Lake. The trip to Pentwater on the steamer *Frontenac*, nicknamed Front and Back, was rough, and Neva and Edgar were among the few passengers who were not seasick. Over the years, the Chapmans shared their love of Bass Lake with many friends, families, and colleagues in education, many of whom became neighbors and fellow resorters at the lake.

Louella Haigh and her new husband, Charles, also honeymooned at Bass Lake in the early 1900s at a cottage known as the Snodgrass Cottage. Dr. Snodgrass had Mr. Bortell, the fisherman of Bortell's Landing, build the cottage from shipwrecked lumber, a good part of it hard maple cast up on the shore after a raging storm. It was painted a bright canary yellow. Legend has it that "Old Man Bortell" was a big man, which explains why he built such large steps to the upstairs.

The cottage had been purchased in 1902 by a group of about fifteen boys from the Central YMCA in Chicago. They called themselves the Central Outing Club. Herbert Immen Lausen was elected as president and Charles Haigh as secretary of the group, and each member paid monthly dues into the treasury so that they might spend their vacations together.

The first year the Central Outing Club group traveled to Bugg House, a resort hotel on Hamlin Lake, and enjoyed two glorious weeks of rambunctious fun and frivolity, complete with pillow fights and water pitchers dumped on each other's heads. The next summer the group planned to return, but Mr. Bugg wrote to them that they were filled up, so the boys sought other accommodations at Hotel McKee on the east side of Bass Lake, applied, and were accepted by Maggie McKee. Apparently, their lively reputation had preceded them, because when they arrived loaded down with all their baggage, Maggie met them with the news that she wouldn't be able to take them in because the cook had fallen down the stairs and broken her leg. Not to be deterred, the boys decided to buy their own cottage and contacted Frank Race, the Oak Park, Illinois, real estate man who had some Bass Lake property and sold them the Snodgrass Cottage.

The boys proceeded to bring a large tent, a dozen durable cots, a dozen dining room chairs, heavy restaurant-style dishes, and kitchen equipment. Lausen recruited his mother and aunt as chaperones and cooks. Then with their girlfriends, and an occasional sister or brother, the members of the Central Outing Club were all set to have a glorious vacation spot for the next several years. Tents were set up alongside the cottage for the boys' sleeping arrangement, while the girls occupied the cottage. A long dining table was set in the dining room, with Mrs. Lausen and her sister cooking splendid meals and the girls assisting by waiting tables and washing dishes.

After a few years, a number of the boys married, and their wives had other places at which they wanted to vacation. Finally, Charles Haigh bought the others' interest, and the couple took over the cottage so that they could share the charm and beauty of Bass Lake with their children. The names of the YMCA boys and their friends who enjoyed the cottage those first years are still inscribed on the stairway of the cottage.

Henry Fred Thiele, who immigrated from Hamburg, Germany, in 1892 and established a real estate company in Austin, Illinois, came to Bass Lake as a hunter around the turn of the century. While the land around Bass Lake was ideal for hunting grouse, small birds, and deer because it was so open after all the logging, Thiele was shocked at how scarred the landscape was after the departure of the loggers who had little regard for aesthetics, and he would write letters home to his family in Germany describing the barren terrain. The Austin Hunt Club, of which Thiele was a member, purchased one lot within what is now Thiele's Addition to Bass Lake Park (certified in 1914). Thiele soon realized others might find the Bass Lake area captivating as well, and he used his real estate skills to begin marketing lots for sale to others. Thiele and his wife, Mary Antonia Svec, honeymooned in 1913 at Wayt's Hotel, located in a settlement along the northwest shore of Bass Lake.

Early Inhabitants

Long before the arrival of the Finches, Gilberts, and Thieles, the area around Bass Lake was occupied by Native Americans from the Algonquin-speaking Ottawa tribe. Through a series of treaties in the 1800s, the US government sought to gain access to the Native American-held lands. In 1858, the government relocated many Ottawa, Chippewa, and Potawatomi tribe members to a new reservation that was six miles wide, twenty-four miles long, and located east of Pentwater.

The Native Americans were still very much a part of Bass Lake in the early days, and the newcomers who arrived there remembered being wary of their new neighbors and their unfamiliar ways and maintained a healthy distance when they were in the area. Soon, however, they learned to share the woods, and both groups coexisted amicably for the most part, but sometimes their paths crossed at unexpected times in unexpected ways.

Harry Hillman III shared his family's encounter on their first trip to Bass Lake in 1905 when his father was just a boy. Harry Sr. had gotten his family set up in tents before going back to Chicago with plans to return the following weekend. The first night that his wife, Augusta Blase Hillman, her son, Harry, and his young cousin, Art Blase, spent in the tents without Harry Sr. started out quietly enough. About midnight, two Native Americans came by looking for another tribe member who had run off with one of their wives and threatened bodily harm. Augusta was terrified and sat up the rest of the night with all the money she had with her stuffed in the bosom of her corset. Art Blase sat on a stump with an ax across his lap, and Harry Jr. sat on another stump with a .22 rifle in ready defense. No harm came to the young family, and the incident didn't dissuade the group from returning to Bass Lake. But it definitely made a lasting impression on a young boy.

When the blueberries were ripe in the summer, the Native Americans would arrive to pick for the market and sell the fruit and their woven baskets. They generally camped at Indian Landing, a shallow bay near present day G Street in the southwest corner of Bass Lake. Since they didn't have fresh water with them, they would help themselves to the nearby cottage wells and, occasionally, blankets and the laundry drying on the clotheslines. The eastern woodland Potawatomi tribe of Native Americans lived near Bass Lake as recently as the 1940s.

Early visitors to Bass Lake often began their travels by boarding a Lake Michigan steamship. One such vessel, *Maywood*, started passenger service to Pentwater in 1906. A few years later, the steamship was repurposed to carry fruit crops from West Michigan to Wisconsin. In this Pentwater Lake photo, notice the building located to the left of *Maywood*. Signs on the building's roof read "Launch Livery" and "Bass Lake Line." The boat livery gave disembarking passengers the option to continue their journey north on Lake Michigan to the Bass Lake Outlet.

Chapter 2
Getting to Bass Lake

In the mid 1800s, the Pentwater Harbor channel was only a shallow stream through which men waded. Charles Mears conceived the idea of dredging out this little stream so lake schooners could come into the mill for loading and unloading. He also built a 660-foot-long pier out into Lake Michigan from the north bank of the channel so that the largest boats on the lake could haul lumber to his yards in Chicago and drop off cargo for the village. The boats arriving from Chicago would tie up at a dock about where the Pentwater Yacht Club is now. In the 1850s, Charles Mears built a ferry transport system to cross Pentwater Lake, and it was used for almost seventy years.

Many of the early visitors to Bass Lake arriving from the greater Chicago area around 1900 had a shorter, more direct route by boat and water (120 miles) or a longer route by train and land (240 miles). Either way, travel was usually done overnight, took at least ten hours, and was no easy feat.

By Boat and Launch

During the summer season in the early 1900s, regular passenger boat service was available from Chicago to Pentwater and Ludington, as well as to ports such as White Lake, Muskegon, and Grand Haven. The Goodrich Steamship Line's big steamer, *Alabama*, took passengers as far as Muskegon, where they transferred to a train for the remainder of the journey to Pentwater. The *Kansas* left Chicago several times a week at 7:00 p.m. and arrived in Pentwater by seven the next morning before continuing to Ludington. Boats making this trek included *Illinois, Iowa,*

The passenger steamer *Frontenac* sailed overnight from Chicago, making stops at several resort towns along the Michigan shore before arriving in Pentwater.

and *Frontenac*. The voyage was not without its perils, and rough seas made even the heartiest souls sick. These boats were all made of wood, and they groaned and screamed loudly in any kind of seaway. The Pentwater channel was not always optimally dredged so that when there were big waves, passengers would feel a scraping shudder when passing over a deep trough as the keel scraped sand on the bottom of the lake. Pentwater Harbor could get very busy with passenger boats, lumber schooners, and steam tugs all trying to reach their final destinations at the same time.

Upon arriving in Pentwater, passengers could hire Captain Cramer, who owned a bait shop and provided boat service for train passengers who needed to get across Pentwater Lake. He could also carry travelers to the Outlet by launch. Captain Cramer was the embodiment of a storied sea captain, complete with a weather-beaten face resembling leather, and a cap and pea jacket. The Bass Lake Outlet was the closest travelers could get by water to the early camps, hotels, and cottages at Bass Lake. Captain Cramer would steam along the Michigan shore, with a rowboat trailing behind, and stop as closely as possible to the shore at the Outlet.

The transfer of passengers and baggage from the launch was nerve-wracking as the passengers stepped precariously into the rowboats, all the while hoping to avoid an unexpected swim in the lake as both boats bobbed in the waves. Once the transfer was completed successfully, the rowboats would carry the passengers up to the Outlet and to their final destination on Bass Lake. This was long before there was a dam at the Outlet, and the channel from the Outlet to Bass Lake was still full of stumps from all of the logging done in earlier years.

If a trip had to be abandoned due to rough seas, travelers would beach their boats and walk the rest of the way. A farmer with a wagon would then be dispatched to the beach to collect the belongings left behind and deliver them to the campsite at Bass Lake.

George Finch recalled one of his family's earliest trips in 1904 to their new cottage on Bass Lake. George's uncle, Ed Wanzer, planned an all-water trip to Bass Lake, starting with *Frontenac* from Chicago to White Lake, where they transferred to the coastal steamer *Carrie Ryerson*. Along the Lake Michigan shore, the boat stopped at every resort along the way. Upon arriving in Pentwater, the group transferred to Captain Nickerson's schooner, *Olivia*, a fifty-foot-long ship with both an iron wind (engine) and sails. *Olivia* set sail for the Outlet, loaded with both families, trunks and baggage, and towing two rowboats behind. After getting as close to the Outlet as the depth of the water would allow, the *Olivia* anchored, and the passengers with all of their belongings anxiously loaded into the rowboats and rowed ashore through the surf. As if this weren't challenging enough, the rowboats then had to be dragged over the sandbar because the Outlet was closed. After crossing the sandbar, the group rowed through the Outlet channel and arrived at their new cottages. The men then returned to the Outlet for the rest of the baggage and a second trip to the cottages. As a seven-year-old boy, George found the whole process thrilling.

Myrtle Race Lattin remembered a long pier being built at the Outlet in 1904 and *Olivia* stopping at that pier on the route from Pentwater to Ludington.

When the boats no longer went in and out of Pentwater, those going to Bass Lake would arrive and depart from Ludington. Prior to arrival, travelers would have to arrange by mail with a local farmer to pick up

The schooner *Olivia* offered pleasure sails on Pentwater Lake as well as transportation to Bass Lake via the Outlet in the early 1900s.

passengers and their baggage at the port and drive the wagon thirteen miles to Bass Lake over rough roads without the benefit of springs, and at a walking pace. Visitors to the port in Ludington in the early 1900s may have been fortunate enough to catch glimpses of Great Lakes schooners before they went out of service completely.

By Train and Wagon

Many resorters made the first part of their annual pilgrimage to Bass Lake on a boat from Chicago to Muskegon and then transferred to a Pentwater-bound train. Rail service to Pentwater started in 1872 with the Grand Rapids and Lakeshore Railroad, which was acquired in 1881 by the Chicago and West Michigan Railway. It then became the Pere Marquette Railway, which served Pentwater from 1899 to 1925, with several trains a day to Muskegon and at least one sleeper car. The train ride was a long, dirty one, and Anna Chapman Endicott remembered her grandmother, Anna Gilbert, describing how all the ladies sat with opened umbrellas to ward off the dust and sand. By the fall of 1925, Pere

Passengers arriving by train had the option of taking a launch, foreground with the flag on the stern, or a ferry across the Pentwater Channel to get into town.

Marquette Railway had discontinued passenger service to Mears, and in 1933, the Mears to Pentwater line was abandoned.

Once travelers reached the railroad terminal on the south side of the Pentwater channel, they had to get across the water to the village of Pentwater. The ferry barge could hold several foot passengers and the depot bus (wagon), which was chained in place in case the horses got spooked. A half-inch wire rope extended across the channel and through two loops on the barge. The ferryman and passengers would pull the ferry across the channel by grabbing the wooden gizmos, and eventually the ferry made it to the other side. The ferryman was responsible for dropping the wire to the bottom of the channel when boats passed to avoid potential disasters, but sometimes he forgot, which caused great problems when incoming boats got snagged. The ferry system was replaced by a swing bridge in 1926.

After crossing the channel, travelers could hire a driver, such as Mr. Eisenlohr, with a buggy and team of horses, or a local farmer, perhaps Mr. Kunsky, who would drive them out to Bass Lake with his horse and wagon. The wagons followed the north-south county road, an unimproved sand track through the woods that was just wide enough for one vehicle, to the Mason-Oceana county line. The sand was very deep, so the horses could travel no faster than a walk and had to be rested often. The road left Pentwater east of the cemetery and went along the west ridge of Rattlesnake Drain Swamp, coming out of the woods about where the Wishing Well is now. The north end of Bass Lake could be reached by going around the east side of the lake or by following the two-track on the west side of the lake and crossing the log bridge over the Outlet channel. Either way, arriving by wagon was a long, hard journey which took hours from Pentwater.

Row Your Boat

The last two options for getting from Pentwater to Bass Lake were either on foot or by rowboat. The rowboats used in the early 1900s were not like the ones we think of today for an afternoon of fishing on a calm lake. Robert Gilbert USCG (ret). remembered the early rowboats: "These were easy-pulling boats which handled well with one oarsman and two oars, or with oarsmen or oarswomen with the power of two pairs [of oars]. They were clinker built with two thwarts for rowers, plus bow and stern seats, and a high bluff bow and stern gave them graceful shear. A wine glass stern and skeg helped to maintain heading. Good buoyancy fore and aft kept things reasonably dry in a moderate surf, as in crossing a sandbar. Some were locally built by Captain Ewald, USCG (ret)."

Bass Lake resorters might have taken friends or family leaving their

The term "clinker" refers to a method of boat building. Lapstrake construction, in which the edges of the hull planks overlap each other, used less wood and required less internal framing, making the boat lighter, faster, and easier to handle. A thwart is the rower's seat onto which an oarlock is attached. This rowboat had a small keel running on the bottom side of the boat and ending in a skeg which helped with steering and keeping the boat straight while moving forward. These clinker boats were durable and flexible, making them ideal in the waves of Lake Michigan.

cottage to Pentwater to catch the afternoon boat by rowing from Bass Lake, through the Outlet, over the sandbars, along the shore of Lake Michigan, and through the Pentwater channel. Passengers and their baggage would likely arrive in Pentwater not as dry as when they left. After bidding their friends farewell as the steamer left the harbor, the "transportation team" would stop by the drugstore soda fountain for a treat before rowing back to the Outlet beach and Bass Lake. The hope was always that the afternoon wind had not increased to the point of building waves and making the trip back too difficult. This method of transportation would also be used as well for going to Pentwater for shopping and visiting.

Harry Hillman III realized many years later that his grandfather, on that first trip to Bass Lake in 1905, was on the cutting edge of a trend that would last for generations. After walking to Pentwater and returning on the ferry to Chicago, "he would then work through the week and return the next weekend for his full vacation, giving the family more time at the lake," recalled Harry. "Therefore, Harry Sr. was probably the first summer-weekend commuter from Chicago, starting a tradition that was to continue for generations." Not an easy trip, but certainly worth the effort.

Wanzer family

A clinker-built rowboat navigates through the Outlet channel near the base of Eagle Top circa 1910.

Motoring: A Daunting Journey

As difficult as it was to reach Bass Lake by boat, train, or wagon, traveling by car was even more grueling. Roads were nothing more than sand, dirt, and gravel. Automobiles were very temperamental and high maintenance, and the poor-quality tires over rough roads would frequently blow out, go flat, and need to be changed en route before continuing the journey. Driving itself was physically demanding, requiring great strength to steer and brake. In spite of the struggle, by 1920, visitors to Bass Lake began "motoring" as a way to reach their favorite summer destination.

Hugh Ramsey, son of Rolla Roy Ramsey and Clara Ethel (Smith Ramsey), was a young boy recovering from rheumatic fever when his parents began to look for a summer vacation spot where Hugh (then twelve years old) could hike, swim, and enjoy the great outdoors. The Ramseys purchased a 1916 Auburn Touring car, their first automobile, and decided to explore some northern Indiana lakes, which they quickly eliminated from consideration. The Ramseys' good friends, Edgar and Neva Chapman, invited them to Bass Lake with assurances that the family would like it, despite the two-day journey from Bloomington, Indiana.

In 1919, the Ramsey family began their 375-mile trek to Bass Lake in the Auburn, which was equipped for touring and camping with a canopy that could be opened up and used as an overnight shelter. Thanks to a friendly farmer, his farm between South Bend, Indiana, and Berrien Springs, Michigan, became the family's regular place to camp overnight, a tradition that continued as they traveled back and forth over the years. Upon arrival at Bass Lake, they set up camp on a vacant lot not far from the Chapmans' cottage, and loved it all—the lake, the surrounding area, the people, and the beach—for it was just what they had been looking for.

In these early years, few people drove to Bass Lake unless it was to position an automobile for their use during the summer. Mrs. Osborne, who lived on a farm just north of Bass Lake, would meet cottagers at the boat in Ludington and drive them as far as her farm because she did not want to risk getting her old Ford stuck in the sand ruts. Her neighbor, Mr. Kunsky, would take the travelers the rest of the way to their cottages with his horse and wagon. If an old Model T happened to bounce into a sandy rut and couldn't get out of it, passengers would exit the vehicle, lift the car back on the traveled path, and resume their trip. The mailman, Mr. Squires, made his deliveries in a Model T with an ooga horn that loudly announced his approach.

In 1911, the vision was cast and promoted for the West Michigan Pike, a well-marked and continuous paved automobile touring route along Michigan's western shore. If motorists could travel more easily on hard surface roads between Chicago and west Michigan, tourism at Michigan's resorts could flourish. As automobile transportation became popular over the next decade, vacationers in their private vehicles were able to reach previously inaccessible remote dune and lakefront destinations such as Bass Lake.

By the 1920s and 1930s, resorters began arriving on the ferries from Chicago with their automobiles. When fathers visited on the weekends and brought their cars, mothers took the opportunity to go into town and do the shopping.

Even though roads improved by the 1930s, travel to Bass Lake by automobile was severely hampered during World War II because of the strict 35-mph speed limit and gas rationing. Many of the Bass Lake regulars were unable to come to the lake from 1942 to 1945. Gas stamps were required to make fuel purchases, and they were difficult to accumulate. Gas rationing was affecting life at Bass Lake in other ways; fuel was needed to run the weed harvester. Harry Hillman reported to the Bass Lake Park Improvement Association in the summer of 1943 that he was able to secure a book of gas coupons from the rationing board to run the weed harvester in Bass Lake. The speed limit restriction and gas rationing were lifted soon after the end of World War II on September 2, 1945.

As roads improved and speed limits increased, people could get to Bass Lake more easily and faster. Highways led to freeways, but often there seemed to be road construction, especially between Bass Lake and Chicago, around "the bottom of the lake." When flying to Grand Rapids or Muskegon became an option, cottagers could arrive from far-flung locations such as California or Florida on the same day they left home. Some cottagers would even leave a car in a garage at Bass Lake over the winter so they wouldn't have to drive back and forth after the summer season.

This woman at the well was Etta Finch Wanzer circa 1905. The Wanzers had built one of the first cottages on the western shore of Bass Lake the previous year.

Chapter 3
Early Cottages and Cottage Life

Bass Lake is a promised land
It is our truest home ... Festooned with memories
Each path and tree and view
The former camp of native peoples ... the feel of them prevails
The land is a living being.

—Jean Gilbert Kraybill

From Tents to Cottages and Cabins

Early visitors to the Bass Lake area had few options as far as
accommodations, and what was available was considered primitive at
best. Unless one rented a room at Wayt's Hotel on the west side of Bass
Lake or at Hotel McKee on the east side, lodging for the night may have
been a tent or one of the old lumber-camp "cabins," which were really
not much more than shanties and often infested with mice, chipmunks,
mosquitos, squirrels, lizards, snakes, and other unwanted pests found in
the woods.

As more families continued to make the trek to Bass Lake each summer
in the early 1900s, efforts began in earnest to make summer dwellings
more permanent than the tents that had been used up until this time.
Between 1905 and 1915, more Bass Lake property owners began to build
simple wooden-frame cottages. By today's standards, the workmanship
on the early cottages may be judged as crude, but it must be remembered
that those first cottages, often built on shoestring budgets, were actually
substitutes for tents, and were considerable improvements.

Early cottages were mostly one-and-a-half story clapboard homes with low-pitched gable roofs, prominent chimneys, and small covered porches. Log cabins featured a simple interior with one room, perhaps partitioned, over which a loft might be built. Cloth netting was placed over cottage windows every year to keep the mosquitos out. Mattresses were filled with straw. Fresh water was pumped by hand from wells. Perishable food was kept chilled underground or in an icebox. Kerosene lamps and candles were used for lighting, and wood was used to fuel the stoves for cooking and warmth. Bathing was done at the Outlet in Lake Michigan. Outhouses were often a short sprint away from the dwelling and often received nicknames such as "The Swiss Village," "Old Barleybreigh," or "The Hoop-de-Doop." Look in the woods around Bass Lake today, especially when the leaves are off the trees, and some of those century-old outhouses can be seen standing today; they may or may not still be used for their original purpose.

Built in 1903, the oldest known cottage on Bass Lake is Karaway Kabin, which was constructed by Wallace Gilbert for his own family and is located in Gilbert's Addition to Bass Lake Park, on the west side of the lake on Bass Lake Boulevard. Justin Elmer "Dut" Bortell and Charlie Bortell helped cut the logs and set them vertically (stockade fashion) with their ends three feet below ground level and the frost line. The

Chapman family

Karaway Kabin is the oldest known cabin on Bass Lake. Wallace B. Gilbert was the original owner, and the cabin remains in the family five generations later.

roof was designed to "split the raindrops."

Wallace Gilbert's enthusiasm for Bass Lake was so contagious that when he suggested to Herman Enders in about 1904 that he construct a cottage for his own family on the ridge behind Karaway Kabin, Mr. Enders, sight unseen, contracted for a cottage to be built by David McKee. Herman and Hattie Enders and their daughters, Lucille and Irene, quickly embraced the Bass Lake way of life. Eventually the Enders built a year-round home closer to the lake, and their original little cottage was sold to Lila and Mae Curtis, who then sold it to Dorothy Smith.

Bass Lake Yell

Hoop-a-la! Hoop-a-la! Rah! Rah! Rah!
The Bass Lake! The Boss Lake!
Yah! Yah! Yah!
A Ki-yi-yi! And a Ku-yu-yu!
If you'd been there,
You'd say so, too!

Neva Gilbert Chapman passed this "yell" down to her family. "Hoop-a-la" became a family greeting to announce your presence upon arrival at the cottage.

Something for Nothing

In the summer of 1903, Edwin T. Wanzer and his young son, Irving, traveled to Bass Lake to see how the Finch family was faring at the church camp, and he liked what he saw. He had been in search of a sandy-bottomed lake, and Bass Lake was just what he'd been looking for. At the time, there were no cottages along the Outlet or south of it to the Oceana County line. The land south of the Outlet was owned by a man named Frank E. Pray, and he was anxious to get some cottages built in hopes of attracting buyers for the property. Mr. Pray had brown hair and a flaming red beard, and Ed repeatedly referred to him as that "pink-whiskered cuss." After much negotiation, Mr. Pray told both Ed Wanzer and Bertha Finch that if they built cottages costing at least five hundred dollars, he would give them each a one-hundred-by-five-hundred-foot lot for free on which to build their cottages. They could choose any place south of the Outlet. Bertha chose a lot with some oak trees and a small knoll on the land, reasoning that there should always be a breeze on the knoll when all else was still, and she was right. Ed chose the property just to the north of Bertha's, and plans were made to build cottages in the spring of 1904.

Sam and George Lake of Hart were typical builders and behind schedule the following spring. When the Finch and Wanzer families arrived in the summer of 1904, the Wanzer cottage had roof rafters but no roof. The Finch cottage had a roof but no doors and windows yet. Both families had to live in the Finch cottage that summer as it was—almost like camping, except without the tent. The group of seven included young George and his older sister, Dorothy, and their mother, Bertha Finch, as well as Bertha's sister-in-law, Etta Wanzer, her husband, Edwin T. Wanzer, and their children, Alice and Irving.

The Wanzer cottage was on 166 feet of waterfront property that extended back about five hundred feet toward the dune, Fairview. A well with a hand pump made from a young tree serviced both cottages. To the west was a "luxurious" (four-holer) outhouse. Built into the dune was a concrete-block cellar that was used to store ice from the winter and cool food in the summer. Eventually a boathouse was built near the shore. A porch extended the full width of the cottage, and was ideal for sleeping, napping, visiting, or for just sitting contentedly and observing the lake. Inside were a living area, a bedroom downstairs, another one upstairs, and a kitchen along the south side of the house. Because the cottage was built in front of a dune, the prevailing westerly breeze was often blocked

> "Sometimes I want to wrap my arms around the cottage and hug it. Sometimes I feel the presence of parents, aunts, cousins, and friends who have shared their love with each other."
>
> —Betty Gilbert Ligon

and prevented good air circulation in the cottage. The importance of this was not lost on young Irving Wanzer. Years later when he and his wife, Amy Rowe Wanzer, built their cottage at the north end of the lake, the site they chose for their cottage was farther from the lake but up on the hill where they could receive a good breeze.

Ready-made

While there were very few dwellings in existence around Bass Lake in the early 1900s, the Ramsey family was fortunate to be able to purchase a cottage that was already built. John Ramsey recalls how the R.R. Ramsey cottage came to be the center of their family summer traditions.

In 1920, the Ramseys purchased their cottage for less than five hundred dollars. The previous owner, Samuel Gamble, was a music teacher who had a piano on the porch and would play on Sunday afternoons for the Protestant campers and cottagers who gathered on stools in front of the cottage. Painted medium-dark maroon with cedar-shake shingles, the cottage consisted of one room upstairs and another downstairs with an old wood-burning stove, a lean-to kitchen on the north side, and a roof over the hand pump and screened-in porch. Privacy curtains enabled the porch to be used as summer sleeping quarters.

That first year, R.R. Ramsey, who paid close attention to his lot lines, was surprised to notice that the structure covering the pump appeared to be over the north property line. Over the winter, a nearby year-round resident had furtively moved the steel stakes to the north and south of his property, making his lot wider. Upon this discovery, Mr. Ramsey purchased three additional lots surrounding his property to build a buffer to protect from further encroachment.

Bass Lake Living in the Early Days

Life at Bass Lake in the early 1900s was simple at best, primitive at worst. Some visitors could not abide by the insects, wildlife, and challenges to daily living. Others embraced the beauty of both the lake and the surrounding woods and loved all it had to offer. In the 1920s and 1930s, children spent idyllic summers at Bass Lake making golden memories, typically spending a month or the whole summer with their mothers or grandparents, while fathers visited on weekends and for annual vacations. Early resorters weren't going to let a few inconveniences hinder their enjoyment of being at Bass Lake. Essential aspects of existence, such as food, clothing, and personal care, all looked very different when the first cottagers arrived at Bass Lake.

Early vacationers recognized the amount of work required daily, especially for the women. To address this concern, one summer around 1900, several families hired a cook to prepare meals for the entire group so that the women would have more time to enjoy their vacations. The resorters even built a log cabin for a dining room and kitchen, which included a low loft where some of the children and older girls would sleep. After one summer, the resorters quickly realized that set times for meals interfered with the vacation itself and all the activities, including fishing and swimming.

Sands and Maxwell ran a large general store and delivered groceries out at Bass Lake by wagon, traveling along the beach for many years until 1920, when their business in Pentwater burned down. Customers could place their orders one day and receive it the next. In addition to groceries, the Sands and Maxwell wagons brought anything else Bass Lakers might need from town, including film, medicine, dry goods, and the mail.

Without the modern conveniences at home, food storage and

Dick Warner

The Bass Lake Grocery Man (a.k.a. Sands and Maxwell) delivered supplies to area residents. Order one day, delivery the next—a century before Amazon.

preparation were simple and uncomplicated, yet sufficient. Shallow wells of perhaps six feet had hand-pump handles and concrete walls with wooden covers made of two-inch planks that could be raised. Food would be placed in jars or other covered dishes and kept cold in the ground near the well that pumped ice-cold water from the ground. A stick with a hook on the end or a peach basket with a sturdy string would be used to retrieve the food that was out of reach low in the ground. Some cottages had a cellar in the ground with shelves on the side to store food to keep it cool. Ice would be cut from Bass Lake in the winter, stacked in layers, and covered with sawdust to store it for use in the summer. Fresh milk, eggs, butter, and produce were readily available from local farmers, and many cottagers would row across the lake to the Judge or Lewis farms to secure these items on a daily basis. In later years, these perishables would be delivered by farmers in their wagons.

Many cottages had iceboxes that were used to keep food cool. Lyman Wayt had an icehouse where nearby resorters could buy a piece of ice and carry it back to their iceboxes. Ice would be delivered several times per week after cottagers put their orders in for how many pounds they needed. Sometimes the ice block would have to be chipped away to make it fit in the icebox. A pan under the icebox collected the melted water, and it would have to be emptied regularly before it overflowed.

Red ants were also a problem, and food had to be covered and protected from the pests. This was accomplished by keeping food on a big swinging shelf on wires.

Woodstoves were used not only for heating, but also cooking, baking, and roasting. Wood had to be chopped for the fire and sometimes fat pine was used to get the fire started faster. Water was heated on the stove, carefully conserved, and used for washing dishes.

When mothers insisted that it was time for children to wash, a pitcher and basin came in handy. Mothers used kettles of hot water and pitchers of cold water to wash and rinse girls' long hair. Early vacationers at Bass Lake often bathed in Lake Michigan at the Outlet.

Kerosene lamps were used for lighting, and every morning the wicks had to be trimmed, and the lamp chimneys had to be washed. Families would read in the evenings around a round-wick kerosene lamp and then use candles to light their way to bed. If matches weren't available or easy to locate, coming home after dark and trying to light a lamp was difficult.

Disposing of garbage was not as easy as waiting for the garbage truck to come by and pick it up or hauling trash to the township dump or transfer site. Most cottagers dug holes and buried their trash, shoveling a little sand on each new addition that was thrown in to keep the flies down. A really deep hole might be big enough to handle the garbage for the whole summer.

The clothing was basic, functional, and low maintenance. Shoes were optional, except for Sundays when it was time to go to church.

By the 1930s, families saw the need to expand their early cottages. Work would often be done by family members, sometimes enlisting the help of the local handyman, Payton Copas. The Ramsey garage was constructed from a Montgomery Ward prefabricated kit. Cottagers enhanced the enjoyment of their waterfronts by adding piers which were relatively short compared with the piers we have today, and often built with simple planking. The piers had to be removed each fall to prevent being damaged by ice in the winter.

Up until this point, there were very few home conveniences, and the basic necessities were often messy and inconvenient. That all changed with the arrival of electricity at Bass Lake.

Electricity first became available at Bass Lake in 1939, thanks to the Rural Electrification Administration, Franklin Delano Roosevelt, and the Hillman family. After figuring what the cost would be to bring electricity to the area, it was agreed that each cottage owner would pay fifty dollars toward the infrastructure required for the service. Because not enough cottage owners initially signed up, there was a shortfall in the funds available. So, Henry Thiele Sr. and Arthur S. Morrison agreed to cover the balance needed with the understanding that they would be paid back as each subsequent cottage accepted electricity.

The Hillman cottage was the first to have light, and the milestone was commemorated by inviting everyone around the lake to come and share in the festive occasion. Electricity changed the way of life at Bass Lake. In the early days, Bass Lake residents didn't feel deprived of luxuries because of the lack of electricity. They accepted things as they were and developed ways to keep food cool, cook, and light or heat their

Roads around Bass Lake in the 1920s and '30s were little more than two-tracks. The Hillman cottage with the stone columns is on the left.

chosen abodes. Cottages could now be modernized—kerosene lamps were replaced with lights that came on with the flick of a switch, and iceboxes were replaced with refrigerators. Cottages got bathrooms with indoor plumbing, complete with electric pumps for running water, indoor toilets, and water heaters that suddenly made bathing in real bathtubs with hot water very easy. Radios replaced Victrolas for musical entertainment and also provided a source for news. Outhouses weren't gone, just not necessary anymore, and they certainly weren't forgotten.

But not everyone was pleased with this modern convenience. Betty Gilbert Ligon wrote that her dad fought hooking up to electricity as long as possible, but her mother loved it. No more looking for matches. No more pumping water by hand. No more trips to the outhouse. No more heating water on the woodstove. Betty exclaimed, "No wonder Mother liked it!"

All Work and Plenty of Play

Even though the introduction of electricity to cottage living made the chores much easier, there was still plenty of work to be done. Young girls typically helped with the cooking and housework, and boys were assigned the outdoor chores such as chopping wood, maintaining boats, and construction projects, often under the watchful eye of a patient grandfather. Hank Thiele recalls that in his youth, the work/play schedule was opposite for girls and boys: the girls did housework in the morning and went to the beach in the afternoon, and the boys went to the beach in the morning and did chores in the afternoon. Hank was fairly confident that this schedule was by design.

The uncomplicated pleasures from the earliest days at Bass Lake seem to be the familiar basis for many of the activities we enjoy today. "It was a simple, clean, healthy way of life. Now I'm grateful that I was privileged to spend my childhood and teenage days up at the lake," Myrtle Race Lattin recalled, referring to the fun she had had as a girl at Bass Lake in the early 1900s. In those days, young people made their own fun, including picnics on Eagle Top, trips and exploring around Bass Lake, and ball games between resorters and Hotel McKee guests. Afternoons were spent at the Outlet, swimming or playing in the sand, and were often followed by a beach supper when the older folks brought the food by boat. "There were simple parties, bonfires, marshmallow roasts, games, and singing. One summer one of the boys had a guitar and we sang our hearts out that year with 'Shine on Harvest Moon' and 'Me and My Gal' and 'I Wonder Who's Kissing Her Now.'"

> "No matter what changes took place from time to time, the charm of the lake was never lost."
> —Gladys McMullin McKevitt

As a youngster in the 1930s, Bob Gannett had many happy memories of endless unplanned activities such as swimming across Bass Lake or at the Outlet beach, sailing, exploring Blueberry Hill and the Three Sisters, his aunt's good meals cooked on the old woodstove, and the wonderfully refreshing ice-cold water from the pump. Later, as a young man, Bob introduced his future wife, Ashley, to Bass Lake, where they enjoyed games on the beach in the evening at sunset, tennis, hiking, swimming, Pentwater Yacht Club dances, and the square dances at Camp Morrison.

Each generation holds special memories of being at Bass Lake and what makes being there special. It's no surprise that many of the same pastimes are often mentioned and have remained consistent for more than a century: picnics at the beach; paddling around in kayaks, canoes, and rowboats; hiking the trails to the beach; picking blueberries, cherries, and apples; napping in a hammock, on a front porch, or on the beach; enjoying the freedom to explore; special equipment at the cottage such as grills, skillets, or stoves; the joy of reuniting with summer friends and playing with cousins; sprucing up the cottage; playing cards or board games in the evening or on rainy days; reading; fishing; swimming; working jigsaw puzzles; chatting or singing around campfires; biking; trying new recipes; seeking out nature; writing letters or postcards; or just daydreaming.

Farmers Market

The Bass Lake area was surrounded by farms that grew all kinds of fresh produce, particularly cherries and blueberries, and the resorters benefitted from all that was available throughout the summer. Farmers and their wives came through the woods, selling their fruit and vegetables, and the Native Americans also picked and sold blueberries, which grew wild in the woods. Resorters would buy or pick enough fruit to can in mason jars which would then be wrapped in newspaper, packed in trunks or barrels fitted with padded tops, and shipped home by freight to enjoy during the winter.

George Finch remembered how fruit was transported in the early days. Every afternoon at 3:30, the small excursion and freight steamer *Lizzie Walsh* was loaded with the fruit that had been harvested that day and then left port, bound for Ludington. Here the fruit was transferred to the black boat, a boat that regularly made the run daily between Milwaukee and Ludington. These boats were passenger boats that carried a lot of freight, not train ferries. Some of these black boats were named *Nevada, Pere Marquette #5,* and *Virginia.* Fruit put on the black boat one day would be on sale the next morning at the Milwaukee wholesale market. As a boy, when George was swimming at the beach, he knew it was time to go home when *Lizzie* was opposite the Outlet.

In the 1970s and 1980s, local Amish from neighboring farms would travel around Bass Lake in their horse-drawn wagons and sell fresh produce and baked goods to the cottagers. The sight of the horses and wagons plodding along Lakeshore Drive offered Bass Lake residents a glimpse into a simpler time. Roadside stands, like the one at the Kistlers' farm, offered passersby the freshest and best of the local cherry harvest.

Even today, the fresh fruits and vegetables are some of the best things about summer at Bass Lake. Cottagers eagerly anticipate the various harvests each month, from cherries to blueberries to corn to apples, with lots of other natural treats throughout the summer. Bass Lakers can take advantage of the local farmers market each week of the summer on the Village Green in Pentwater or stop at nearby farm markets. The wild blueberries around Bass Lake aren't nearly as plentiful as they were a hundred years ago, but cottagers look forward each summer to picking their own blueberries at U-pick farms such as the Pentwater Patch. In

"THE WISHING WELL" — FRUITS AND GROCERIES — PENTWATER, MICH.

Pentwater Historical Society

Conveniently located along Business US Highway 31, the Wishing Well gas station and convenience store has been a familiar landmark in the Bass Lake community since the 1940s. At one time, it was one of the few places Bass Lake residents and visitors could place phone calls.

these more modern times, fresh produce is frozen, packed in freezer bags, and transported home in coolers for enjoyment throughout the year.

Times Change

Things changed in the 1940s with America's involvement in World War II. Bass Lake did not escape the profound impacts of the war. Fathers were shipped off to war, young men were drafted or enlisted, essential items were rationed, and travel was difficult. Families waited anxiously to hear from their loved ones. In their letters home, many of the young men who had enjoyed previous carefree summers at Bass Lake would write of their longing to be back at Bass Lake and what they would do there when the war was over and they returned. Many families who routinely spent the summer at Bass Lake did not return for a few years, and some not at all.

As members of the Greatest Generation grew up, launched careers, got married, and started families, they would continue the tradition of Bass Lake summers, often just a week or two at a time. The family cottages were bursting at the seams with expanding families as future spouses and more children and grandchildren were introduced to the tradition of summers at Bass Lake. Everyone wanted to be at the cottage at the same time, especially for the Fourth of July and Pentwater Homecoming weekend in August. To accommodate the overflow, cots were added to porches, tents were pitched, extra cottages were rented, or campers brought in. Cousins reunited during blissful days at Bass Lake, and longtime friends met up at the beach, on a boat, on a front porch, or around a campfire.

In the 1960s and 1970s, more mothers went to work outside the home and couldn't spend entire summers at Bass Lake unless they were educators and on summer break.

Adult siblings began to share time in the family cottages when parents and grandparents were no longer making the annual

> "No matter how far-flung the members of the family are, the one place that draws everyone together is Bass Lake."
> —Harry Hillman III

pilgrimage to Bass Lake. As this group moved toward retirement in the 1980s, many wanted to spend more time at Bass Lake and began to build new cottages on existing family land or bought other cottages nearby. Some older cottages were starting to be torn down and replaced with new, more modern structures that could accommodate more family members. Air conditioning became standard in new builds, and some older cottages were retrofitted with air cooling systems, which made the old metal fans obsolete and faded the familiar, musty cottage smells. After the devastating high-water year of 1986, many cottagers added seawalls to protect their shorelines. Short wooden docks were replaced with newer, longer piers, many made of metal and composite materials. Some wooded yards that had been dotted with wild ferns were replaced with manicured lawns.

As time marched on into the 1990s and 2000s, children didn't seem to have the carefree summers that their parents and grandparents had had in decades past. Schools went later in the spring or started earlier in the summer, often before Labor Day. Sports activities took priority with seasons extended well into summer, while high school sports practices started as early as August 1. Themed camps and other enrichment activities competed with leisurely unscheduled days of wandering through the woods at Bass Lake or playing for hours at the beach until the sun set. Summer jobs and college internships drew young adults away from summers at Bass Lake.

Suddenly, everything changed in 2020 when the world shut down because of the coronavirus pandemic. Bass Lake never looked so good. Anyone with a previous connection to the area was immediately drawn to the sunshine and fresh air, walks in the woods and on the beach, open windows, open spaces, and a less dense population. Many jobs became remote, and other activities were canceled or became virtual. A generation who had never had an opportunity to spend an extended period of time at Bass Lake suddenly had the whole glorious summer spread out before them. And as was the case for over a hundred years, Bass Lake did not disappoint.

The Cottage
1.
In the woods,
Thick with brush
On the ridge
Where the thrush
Sings his flute-like
Melody of love.

2.
You will find
A cottage camp
Near the lake
A morning's tramp
From the village
In the hills.

3.
Spot of pleasure
Place of joy
Of happiness without alloy
Is the cottage
On the ridge.

4.
Realm of rest
In the brush
On the ridge
Where the thrush
Sings his flute-like
Melody of love.

—Irving Haight Wanzer
(circa 1910)

Hotel McKee was the first of its kind on Bass Lake's eastern shore and drew visitors from Chicago. It's believed the land was previously owned by lumber baron Charles Mears in the 1800s.

Chapter 4
Restful Resorts

As the Mason County and Oceana County lumber industry waned, interest renewed in property surrounding Bass Lake. Savvy individuals endeavored to develop properties that appealed to all sorts of people. By the early 1900s, hotels, cottages, and camping resorts dotted the shorelines. In some cases, names have changed—Camp Morrison became Whispering Surf and Call's Resort transformed into Ferwerda's Bass Lake Resort. Beckoning restful resorts have become summer abodes to visitors and renters who often return to Bass Lake year after year, escaping to a laid-back lifestyle for a few relaxing days, weeks, or months.

Hotel McKee / Schlick's Resort / Smert's Resort on Bass Lake

George C. McKee was a Summit Township boy living east of Bass Lake on the family farm. He purchased thirty acres on Bass Lake's eastern shore, and by the very early 1900s, George had a seventeen-room hotel fronted by wide sitting porches for the new influx of tourists. He and his older sister, Margaret "Maggie" McKee, ran Hotel McKee, which included several cabins and a "floating" dance pavilion. "We children loved to row across the lake to Margaret McKee's hotel," wrote Anna Chapman Endicott, whose family owned Karaway Kabin on Bass Lake's west shore. "A pavilion extended over the water with room for boats under the floor. We used to run around the floor and climb on the benches surrounding it to look out the windows with their awning-type shutters."

George deeded his hotel to Maggie in 1915. Then in 1920, Hotel McKee

Early in its history, Hotel McKee had a unique dance pavilion on a pier extending into Bass Lake. Resorters from all around the lake would come to socialize.

was sold to Chicago residents Erva and Tom Schlick, who decided to leave Chicago for a healthier life in Michigan. The couple renovated the building and created Schlick's Resort, a small hotel with a huge dining room, twelve rockers on the screened porch, and eight cottages. In 1928, Tom passed away, leaving his wife and son, Claude, to run the resort. Claudia Schlick Goudschaal remembered her grandmother had the only telephone and mailbox on the east side of Bass Lake. As a child, Claudia was oftentimes enlisted as mail carrier and phone page, which usually earned her a nickel or dime to spend in town.

In 1972, Lea and Vince Smiertelny bought Schlick's Resort. They renamed it Smert's Resort on Bass Lake. A circa-1973 information-packed leaflet advertised: "Stay in a Turn-of-the-Century cottage on beautiful Bass Lake. Smert's Resort is a land of unexcelled rustic grandeur, bright sunny days, and fresh cool evenings extending to spectacular sunsets at 10 p.m. Here you can enjoy fishing, boating, swimming, water skiing, sailing, or just relaxing in the health-giving fresh air."

The Smiertelnys not only ran Smert's Resort, in 1980 Lea opened her own real estate company, Three Lakes Realty & Land Co.

By 2017, the resort fell into disrepair, and the Smiertelnys sold the property to a private buyer. A May 2017 estate sale gave the public the opportunity to own a piece of Bass Lake resort history. Anything you found at the former Smert's Resort and could carry out was for sale, including doors and windows. Soon after the sale, the new owner razed the site and returned the property on the eastern shore of Bass Lake to its natural, peaceful state.

Wayt's Hotel: A Beautiful, Quiet Place in the Woods

Lyman H. Wayt advertised his early-1900s hotel situated on the scenic road on the west shore of Bass Lake, as follows: "Wayt's Hotel is pleasantly situated on the west shore of the lake in a grove of young pine and oak, within easy walking distance of Lake Michigan. The rooms are clean, airy, and well-furnished. An atmosphere of homelike freedom and comfort provides the place with none of the former chill of public houses. It is a place where a sojourn, long or short, may be spent with fullest enjoyment. It does not claim to be equal in all its appointments to the first-class hotels of cities, but it does give attention to cleanliness and orderly care and attention [is] given to rooms and bedding." The hotel opened for the season on June 15. Room rates were two dollars per day or eight to ten dollars per week, depending on the number of occupants. Lyman, his wife, Helen, and their three children (Gervin, Robert, and Miriam) all pitched in to run the hotel. Even playmates helped.

Anna Chapman Endicott, who spent summers a few cottages north of Wayt's Hotel, felt it was a fascinating place with much activity. She would help her friend Miriam with her chores, such as setting tables in the big dining room and answering the tap bell when a guest wanted something at the counter near the front door. One day, Gervin caught a huge turtle, and the hotel cook made turtle soup for the guests. But Anna said she couldn't taste it after watching the creature be beheaded.

The summer hotel touted that home cooking was a specialty, with daily supplies of cream, milk, butter, eggs, fruits, and vegetables. It was

Wayt's Hotel and summer cottages on Bass Lake's western shore offered Bass Lake resorters all the comforts of home. It was a hub of activity in the early 1900s.

considered the center of activity and housed the first post office on the west side of Bass Lake. Many newlyweds honeymooned at the hotel. The Wayts also rented summer cottages.

Area visitors could buy chunks of ice at the hotel to use for refrigeration. Cut from Bass Lake in the winter, the ice was covered with sawdust and stacked in layers in the Wayt's icehouse to keep for the summer months.

Besides being a hotel proprietor, Lyman was a carpenter, real estate investor, surveyor, lighting equipment salesman, and 1915 treasurer for the Bass Lake Park Improvement Association. Sadly, Lyman died February 22, 1932. While crossing Bass Lake with his surveying equipment, the sixty-three-year-old man fell through the winter ice and drowned. By 1937, the hotel was no more, and the property was sold to the Otto Linneman family.

Camp Morrison / Whispering Surf Campground

Arthur "Morrie" Morrison, an enterprising theologian, had the foresight to establish a resort at Bass Lake before there were public campgrounds and before there was even a true road to Pentwater. Morrie had the charisma and personality to make guests happy and want to come back. The primitive new resort had its fair share of setbacks over the years but came alive during the 1920s and was transformed over time.

First used as a church choir camp, Camp Morrison opened in 1913 and during those early years guests truly roughed it. The lodging was tents. Guests cooked over open fires. After traveling to Pentwater by steamship or train, they took a boat to the Bass Lake Outlet, then walked to the camp. By 1927, with the help of Morrie's wife, Georgia "Nana" Morrison, services included meals to guests in a newly constructed pavilion. Also, that year a new dam was constructed at the Outlet to help maintain the lake level, which greatly improved the condition of the lake for recreation. Fish were abundant, and boating was popular. Even

A typical Camp Morrison menu might feature the following:

Saturday, June 24, 1948

LUNCH
Homemade Chicken Noodle Soup ... 20 cents
Cube Steak Special ... 75 cents
Creamed Chicken à la King on Biscuit ... 65 cents
Pan Fried Fillet of Perch ... 65 cents

DINNER
Grilled Pork Chops or Grilled Sirloin Steak with Peas, Carrots & Potatoes ... 75 cents
Spaghetti with Tasty Meat Sauce and Hot Biscuits & Butter ... 50 cents
Homemade Pie ... 17 cents
Ice Cream Sundae ... 25 cents

THANK YOU ~ COME AGAIN!

during the Great Depression, Camp Morrison flourished as a reasonably priced resort. In the 1930s, the road around the west side of Bass Lake was improved, making it easier to come and go.

A 1950s brochure advertised the unique charms of Camp Morrison:

The best guarantee we can give you is that 90 percent of all those who have come here for the first time have returned. When you vacation at Morrison's Resort, you're in Bass Lake Dune Country where you can roam through the twenty acres of oak and pine forest on our property. Swim and relax, enjoy the sloping beach of Lake Michigan. Bass Lake is connected to Lake Michigan by a scenic, winding outlet. Cottages have been built on the extensive grounds with plenty of room and privacy. Morrison's Resort is the active community center. For your comfort: innerspring mattresses, comfortable furniture, well-screened windows, wood burning stoves for heating if it is necessary. For convenience: running water and modern flush toilets. You don't need a car—we will meet you when you arrive at the Greyhound Station Bus Line Stop off US 31 just a mile away. Folks in Chicago can take the train to Milwaukee and board the ferry to Ludington.

Many who visited the camp recall with fond nostalgia attending summer square dances in the pavilion. Camp Morrison officially closed in 1958. But in July and August 1965, its pavilion briefly reopened with a snack bar two nights per week for teen dance parties.

Stories and rumors of what went on at Camp Morrison included availability of bootleg alcohol, gambling, and gangsters from Detroit or Chicago. One of the more touching stories is of entertainers Bea and Billy Walsh. While in the same vaudeville unit in 1918 Chicago, Billy met Bass Lake resorter Edward Tallman, who already owned property. After several visits, eventually Billy had a cottage. Billy and his wife, Bea, entertained residents during summers at Bass Lake. Their famous vaudeville act was performed at Camp Morrison. Then in 1946 while overseas with the USO to entertain World War II troops, their plane crashed in the Pacific Ocean. They were never found. Bass Lake residents mourned the loss of their friends. In remembrance, a memorial stone and plaque were placed under a large white pine across from the Wishing Well at the south end of Lakeshore Drive. In 1996, the memorial stone and plaque were moved to

Historic White Pine Village south of Ludington.

Eventually, resorts like Morrison's faced competition from more modern lodging—motels, bed and breakfasts, and more upscale resorts. Some longtime vacationers opted to rent or buy single-family cottages around Bass Lake.

In 1966, Reginald Yaple purchased the shuttered Camp Morrison. His vision was to capitalize on the burgeoning recreation vehicle (RV) business by converting the property into a summer campground. He renovated the property to make it accessible for modern RVs and renamed the resort Whispering Surf Travel Trailer Village.

Today Whispering Surf Campground at Bass Lake, operated by Lisa Manning and Fred Manning, is the oldest privately owned campground in Michigan. It offers tent and RV campsites, as well as cottages. Vacationers can stay for one night or through the entire summer. Many park their RVs at the campground for the entire summer season, outfitting outdoor spaces

Dick Warner

Camp Morrison's pavilion, seen here in the 1940s, was at the center of campground activities. Resorters eagerly anticipated the Saturday night square dances and swing dances, a mainstay of Bass Lake social life for decades. Morrie Morrison touted his campground's availability of cabins, good food, good beds, and a never-to-be-forgotten good time!

Bass Lake Song
(as sung at Camp Morrison to the tune "Hail to Our Alma Mater")

Verse 1
Behind the bluffs of wave-tossed Michigan,
Lies a lake so fair;
That he who sees its green-clad shoreline,
Forgets every care.

Chorus
Bass Lake, Bass Lake, how we love thee,
And the Outlet dear
Our vacations we will spend there,
This and every year.

Verse 2
In the middle of the wild wood,
Lies Camp Morrison,
Where we laugh, and dance, and frolic,
And have lots of fun.

Verse 3
On the Beach or in the Woodland,
We one family are,
Making friends to last a lifetime,
Though we travel far.

Verse 4
Through the years the happy memories
Of these carefree days,
Will brighten dark and bitter moments,
Cheering us always.

with grills, tents, and patio furniture. The atmosphere is of a traditional multigenerational cottage enclave.

Camp Morrison's original Pines Pavilion was rechristened the Lodge and is still the camp's focal point of family events and rainy-day activities. The weathered pine rafters in the vaulted ceiling hint at its dance hall days, and a hand-built 1940 foosball table in the corner could no doubt tell a few good stories.

Call's Resort / Ferwerda's Bass Lake Resort

When Camp Morrison closed in 1958, Robert and Edith Call purchased about four acres of the campground's property. This included lake frontage and nine housekeeping cabins. The cabins were modernized and moved closer to the lake, just east of Whispering Surf campground. Call's Resort became a family vacation compound on the lakeshore.

In 1970, Bob and Betty Watson purchased Call's Resort. The Watsons constructed four additional cabins and built the Hungry Dragon in 1973—a game room and snack bar that fed visitors for many years. Debbie Wlodarski remembered eating the best French fries and hot dogs at the Hungry Dragon. On special occasions her family would boat over to get ice cream. Some of Jay Shiff's fondest memories are of playing video games, pool, air hockey, the jukebox, and pinball at the Hungry Dragon. "It was the gathering place for all the kids," he said.

In the early 1970s, a special group of four families nicknamed the SHaRPs (Schlenker, Handrock, Rosenwinkle, and Pepich) regularly spent one week each summer at Call's Resort. "We'd ski in the morning, and while we waited our turn, we'd chase each other with the paddle boats. We'd spend afternoons at the big lake eating junk food, climbing to the top of Sand Mountain, and sneaking to Peter Pan Land. In the evenings we'd hang out at the Hungry Dragon, playing cards or the latest arcade game," Beth Handrock Walden shared. The SHaRP kids also played shenanigans. Under the cover of night, the group would put the outdoor cabin furniture on the raft, along with the rowboats. They always had fun and ended the week by making their annual human pyramid.

In 1977, the Watsons sold the resort to their nephew on his wedding day. Dave and Laurie Ferwerda renamed it Ferwerda's Bass Lake Resort. It's now managed by the next generation, Kevin and Christen Ferwerda. More than a dozen cabins are available for rent, with romantic names like Cozy Nook and Restful Haven. Many renters return for the same week each year to reunite with family and friends.

Auld Lang Syne

Among the cottage resorts at Bass Lake was Auld Lang Syne, originally named Waldesruh and owned by Clara Parbs. Located near the Bass Lake channel bridge on Lakeshore Drive, Auld Lang Syne was a charming collection of four cottages with small kitchenettes, bathrooms, and a community shower house. The cottages were named Fly-A-Way, Moonbeam, Glow Worm, and Willow—so named for songs of the day.

In 1947, Carl and Loretta Carlson purchased Auld Lang Syne, as well as the Parbs's house. Then in 1965 they sold the business to their daughter, Rochelle "Rocky" Holmes, and her husband, Richard. Many

Dick Warner

Fly-A-Way cottage was one of four Auld Lang Syne cottages welcoming resorters to a restful stay near Bass Lake's channel to the Outlet. In 1947, Carl and Loretta Carlson purchased the cottages which were known by whimsical names: Fly-A-Way, Moonbeam, Glow Worm, and Willow.

of the same guests came year after year, making for a warm coming and going of familiar faces. Rocky's son, Randy Holmes, enjoyed every day of every summer on Bass Lake. He said, "Life was ideal and free from anxiety. Our home was also an annual gathering place for our extensive family to celebrate the Fourth of July. Downsizing in about 1971, my parents closed Auld Lang Syne as a business. But it remains a gathering place for family and loved ones to this day. It's our little slice of heaven."

Fly-A-Way and Moonbeam are now connected by an addition to create a much larger, more comfortable family cottage. And in remembrance of Randy's mother and her love for Bass Lake and its community, Auld Lang Syne is named Camp Rocky. Still, as you boat westward into the Bass Lake channel, you can see the Glow Worm and Willow cottages, as well as the community shower house—all maintained in loving memory of family.

Niles Bass Lake Resort

In the 1950s, Niles Bass Lake Resort was located on the east side of Bass Lake. It included cabins rented by Claude and Carol Niles at the corner of Pere Marquette Highway and Marrison Road. Interest grew in the undeveloped land. The area was subdivided and lots sold, making way for new families wanting to build cottages. Debbie Wlodarski's father, Jim Kelly, his sister, and many friends purchased lots along Lake Street off Marrison Road. And in the 1960s, her parents helped build and expand cottages in the area.

Greene Acres

In the 1960s, several Bass Lake cabins, known as Greene Acres, were rented by the Greene family at the end of Park Avenue. Ruth Shiff had been coming to Bass Lake since she was a teenager. While she and her husband, George, were looking for a place to live in Evanston, Illinois, they stumbled on a listing for two cabins at Greene Acres. They decided to buy the cabins even before purchasing their Evanston home. Ruth enjoyed being at the cabin so much that she went to nearby Hart, Michigan, for the birth of her son, Jay Shiff. He was at the Outlet when he was one week old. He, his sister, and brother would come to the cabin every summer from the day after school was over until Labor Day. Jay recalled, "Mom would pack the car on the last day of school, the next day load us up in the car at four o'clock in the morning, and off we went. I loved going to the Outlet in the evening with my family and the Giffens, having a bonfire, watching the sunset, roasting marshmallows, and telling jokes."

"Bass Lake, I had been told, was the only place to spend a vacation."
—Marie Hillman

Chapter 5
The Outlet

The Outlet

The weedy, twisted outlet
Where the big-mouth black bass lie,
The wooded, heaped-up sand hills
That rise dark against the sky.

In June the swollen waters
Rush out to the old Big Lake,
And the twisting turbid currents
A thousand channels make.

It is then we pack our outfit
With rod and gaff and fly,
And journey to the Northland
Where the big-mouth black bass lie.

—Irving H. Wanzer (circa 1915)

The Bass Lake Outlet to Lake Michigan is a picturesque spot along Lake Michigan's shoreline between Pentwater and Ludington. It is a treasured destination that attracts beachgoers young and old, year after year. "One of Lake Michigan's finest sugar sand beaches can be found where the Bass Lake Outlet stream flows over a small dam into Lake Michigan," touts a vintage postcard.

While reachable by land or Lake Michigan, a favorite route to the

Outlet is by water along the narrow, scenic channel from Bass Lake. Respecting the peace and quiet of cottagers along the way, one carefully navigates under the Troll Bridge and is greeted by a gnome on one side and Wild Thing on the other. Kayakers and paddleboarders glide into the channel, where its winding glory unfolds—a quarter mile of twists and turns with fallen logs to navigate, sunning turtles, lush native plants, and industrious black squirrels along the shoreline. The reward at journey's end is the sandy beach where humble Bass Lake and stunning Lake Michigan become one.

Dick Warner

This circa 1900 wooden bridge was built over the channel that connects Bass Lake to Lake Michigan. The bridge was a vital link to expand access from the southern to northern areas of the lake. Bass Lake resorters would navigate under the channel bridge to reach the Outlet and Lake Michigan.

The Outlet for All to Enjoy

Not all visitors to Bass Lake know that summers at the Outlet beach are made possible mainly due to the generosity of the Henry Fred Thiele family. Today, the beach property is owned by the Thiele and Woeltje families but leased for public use by Summit Township of Mason County, Michigan.

In 1913, Henry, a real estate salesman from the Chicago area, purchased property for Thiele's Addition to Bass Lake Park, which included land on both sides of the Bass Lake channel all the way to Lake Michigan. Henry subdivided the acreage, built four cottages, and put lots up for sale. His brochure's sales pitch enticed others to Bass Lake:

> *So you need a vacation and a rest. Let me show you a resting place located on the shores of our beautiful Lake Michigan and the Bass Lake Outlet. My sub-division contains about 70 acres. I now offer about 50 building sites for sale, all large water forest lots. This ground is high and has an elevation from 10 to 40 feet above the water line. We have drinking water taken from wells, which is cool all summer and very refreshing. We have a bathing beach with shallow water and a clear sand bottom; there is nothing finer in the country. The climate cannot be surpassed, as the lake breeze always cools the air, so we don't know a hot day at Bass Lake.*

Resorters from all around Bass Lake enjoyed the Outlet swimming beach. In the early days, "One always dressed at the beach. If you came home in a wet bathing suit, you could catch your cold," wrote George B. Finch. He described a Ladies' Beach House, located about twenty-five feet south of the present dam. The structure was made of logs and was about thirty feet square. There was no roof. Inside, it was divided into small cubicles that had no door. Each lady had one of these in which to dress and put on long stockings, bloomers, and a long-sleeved blouse and hat. This is how ladies dressed for "bathing." At one time, there was also a Men's Bathhouse made of sawn board, but it got blown away.

As described by George, early photos show beachgoers wearing modest swimming suits that would not become transparent when wet—usually made of a heavy fabric like wool. Anna Chapman Endicott wrote about the attire worn by her grandmother, who loved to go into Lake Michigan even if it was very cold and nobody else would go in. "I can remember seeing her so well in her black bathing suit, with blousy sleeves and blousy pants, black stockings, and a little black ruffled cap. Maybe that costume helped keep her warm."

Besides the dressing booths, Outlet conveniences at various times included a wooden-plank walkway down the entrance dune, a wooden walkway bridging the Outlet, a water pump, and at some point, a slide.

Back then, these were maintained by the Bass Lake Park Improvement Association (BLPIA), whose early mission included maintaining an orderly and clean bathing beach along with overseeing the dam at the Outlet.

Fun at the Beach

Many families recall daylong visits to the swimming beach, complete with old-fashioned picnics and dinners cooked over a campfire. In the 1920s, Anna Chapman Endicott and her two sisters decided to sleep on the beach. They hollowed out comfortable places to sleep in the sand. Then the next morning, they walked north up the Lake Michigan beach to Bortell's Fisheries (today's Summit Park), where they found Dut and Charlie Bortell preparing to launch their boat. The girls joined them for fishing. Pretty soon, they were covered with fish as Dut and Charlie dumped their catch into the boat, not a container. The girls regretted their overnight adventure on the beach. No doubt other Bass Lake families have tales to tell of overnights on the beach.

For one hundred years, the Behr family has enjoyed their family getaway on the Bass Lake channel. Chris Torp Payleitner described life near the

Going to the "bathing beach" in the 1930s meant wearing conservative swimming attire. Women in dresses and men in suits were not an uncommon sight, either.

Outlet like this: "For all generations, days were spent with lifelong friends and family on the beach. So many hours spent in various types of boats looking for turtles, sailing, and getting sunburned. Skinny dipping, and wearing poison-ivy clothes afterwards, were also possibilities ... How many times did everyone dig the Outlet channel out or watch satellites go by overhead while looking for shooting stars? We still go out as a family to watch the sunset, look at stars and planets, and search the beach for treasured rocks."

The Lasting Thiele Legacy

Henry Fred Thiele's family always enjoyed coming to Bass Lake. His son, Henry Frank Thiele, recalled, "When we got to the cottage, we would take off our shoes and wouldn't put them on until Sunday, when we went to church. There was no electricity in the cottage. The only telephone near us was at Camp Morrison. We made our money by catching frogs to sell to fishermen, and we would catch fish out of the river for our lunch."

Henry Frank Thiele's son, Henry B. "Hank" Thiele, spent a month every summer at Bass Lake with his grandparents from the time he was about five years old. His "run" was from Eagle Top to the bridge over the Bass Lake channel. Not many adults were around on weekdays because fathers were away at work. They came to Bass Lake on weekends.

For decades, the Thiele and Woeltje families' contributions and support have helped sustain the Bass Lake way of life. Their leadership roles in the property owners' association, involvement in the Bass Lake community, and oversight of the Outlet and dam have been key.

In recognition of Henry Frank Thiele's decades of dedication and service, in 2011 a plaque bearing his name was placed on the dam at the Outlet. The Bass Lake community attended a ceremony honoring him and his family for their efforts to maintain the dam, which keeps Bass Lake intact. Kyle Chapman, vice president of the Bass Lake Property Owners Association at the time, credited Henry for being the "voice that guided us" by always advocating for Bass Lake—speaking from experience, and at times, standing up during an association meeting to get the group on task to care for the lake.

Those Darn Dams

One critical aspect of caring for Bass Lake is managing the water level. Water enters it from three creeks—Kibby, Quinn, and Rattlesnake—as well as artesian springs and rain. Too much water in the lake can cause flooding. Too little water impacts recreation, fishing, and the general health of the lake.

As interest in property at Bass Lake grew, so did the desire to maintain the lake's water level. One of the earliest recollections of a dam goes back to the late 1860s, when Martin S. Perkins operated a sawmill on the Bass Lake channel. He built a log dam to raise the water level to float logs; however, log dams did not last long.

In the early 1900s, keeping the inland lake full for fishing and recreation could be a challenge. If the lake level got too low, an appeal would be made for folks to help close the Outlet. "I remember when we had a strong storm, the sand at the Outlet would wash out, and Bass Lake would start draining into Lake Michigan. The residents would go down to the Outlet and try to block it so we didn't lose the lake; that was taken care of in about 1927, when the dam was built," recalled ninety-four-year-old Henry Frank Thiele in 2008.

When the Bass Lake Park Improvement Association was formed in 1915, discussion started right away regarding a dam. By 1916, a dam was built for five hundred dollars and guaranteed to last. But it only lasted one season—again leaving Bass Lake water levels to the whim of Mother Nature. Repairs were made in 1917.

For decades now, the remedy that has worked well to manage Bass Lake water levels is a small dam, called a weir, at the Outlet. It's said that two concrete dams have been built by the BLPIA. Rebar for the first concrete dam was metal bed frames used for reinforcement. This didn't hold up, requiring removal of the center section of the dam and leaving the concrete "wings." The second concrete dam was located upstream of the first and in a much better position to survive. Over the years, repairs have been made to that dam, under the watchful eye of the property owners' association and the Thiele and Woeltje families.

Once a successful concrete dam was built, the water level of Bass Lake stabilized and became more consistent for recreational activities. Yet, nature still plays a role in the water level, as storms like the one in 1986 can wreak havoc and cause flooding.

In the mid-1920s, the Bass Lake Park Improvement Association built a more reliable concrete dam. Peg Van Hook stands in front of the dam on the walkway bridge over the Outlet. "Sidewalks" made of boards were provided down the entrance dune and along the Outlet. Dressing booths were available for changing in and out of swimming attire.

Chapter 6
Time to Organize

A friendly debate sometimes arises at Bass Lake. When did the association representing property owners actually begin? A vintage copy of the *Bass Lake Property Owners Association Constitution and By-Laws* claims the organization dates back to the early 20th century, and although the organization has had a few name changes, it has been in continuous operation since 1915. Yet another vintage copy might say it has been in continuous operation since 1885. So which is it?

MEMBERSHIP CARD

BASS LAKE PARK
IMPROVEMENT ASSOCIATION

This is to certify that

R. Collins

is a member in good standing for the year indicated hereon

1944   Alice B. Finck

SEC'Y

History Committee

In the 1940s, Bass Lake Park Improvement Association members received membership cards. A BLPIA membership decal was also available to display on cottage doors and windows.

The Bass Lake Recreation Park Association came about in the mid-1880s, when three prominent Pentwater residents—William Ambler, Dr. George Cleveland, and Martin Perkins—decided to establish a recreational resort. They sold shares set at twenty-five dollars each to those interested in using the new resort area just north of Pentwater. In 1886, the seventy-seven-acre Bass Lake Recreation Park was ready for resorters interested in fishing, boating, swimming, croquet, and nature. More and more people came to Bass Lake. This led to the need for communal oversight of its ongoing development.

Bass Lake Park Improvement Association

By 1890, the first two Bass Lake summer cottages were built, with more on the way as enterprising land developers purchased acreage, promoting its beauty and affordability. The need for better roads, an improved Bass Lake Outlet dam and other considerations brought a group of twenty-eight Bass Lake property owners together on July 24, 1915, at Lena J. Broomell's cottage.

During the meeting, a not-for-profit structure was agreed to, as well as the name Bass Lake Park Improvement Association (BLPIA). A.H. Conrad was voted president; Edgar K. Chapman, vice president; Lena J. Broomell, secretary; and Lyman H. Wayt, treasurer.

In his maiden speech, the association's new president emphasized that "the keynote of our success is in cooperation, that all sides of the lake are to be considered, and that which is the greatest good to the most people is what we should strive for." It should be noted that association officers and committees were unpaid positions. The same is true today. Everyone is a volunteer.

Early on, many matters came before the BLPIA. Passable roadways were key to accessibility and development. How to manage Bass Lake's water level with a dam at the Outlet to Lake Michigan was ever challenging. Caretaking of cottages in the off-season was key—a three-dollar-per-cottage job was first given to early hotel owners George McKee on the east side of the lake and Lyman Wayt on the west side. Safety, fire protection, sanitation, zoning, and keeping the lake stocked with game fish were important. Financing the newly created BLPIA and growing its membership were paramount to success.

Dealing with concerns and keeping the peace could be challenging. Upon being voted BLPIA's 1942 president, Irving Wanzer told of coming to Bass Lake for the past forty years, since boyhood. And while people residing around Bass Lake were not always of the same opinions, the bond that kept them together was the love of the beauty and surroundings of Bass Lake.

In 1943, members received BLPIA stickers to proudly display on their doors, as well as membership cards. Effort was made to know your neighbors and help when you could.

Bass Lake Property Owners Association

On August 22, 1964—not to announce a shift in the organization's makeup or purpose—the BLPIA's name changed to what we know today, Bass Lake Property Owners Association (BLPOA). This was done to satisfy the requirements of the State Rules of the Michigan Corporation and Securities Commission.

In 1965, the association celebrated its fiftieth anniversary with a gala dinner at the Pentwater Yacht Club. Presiding over the event were officers H.H. Carstens, president; H.A. Tate, vice president; Marie Hillman, secretary; and Mrs. K.C. Barrons, treasurer. Herbert Behr presented "The Four Seasons of Bass Lake."

In 2025, with membership representing more than 260 properties, the BLPOA celebrates its 110th anniversary—a true testament to its persevering leadership, spirit of cooperation, and positive influence for good.

Bass Lake Improvement Board

The Bass Lake Improvement Board (BLIB) is different from the BLPOA. Here's how it came about.

For decades, Bass Lake property owners have battled lake weeds to keep them in check for the sake of recreation, while not impacting natural habitat. Living in harmony is challenging. Making things worse, by the mid-1960s invasive non-native plant life came to Michigan lakes.

The BLPOA was in charge of weed management, consisting mainly of using a weed-cutter machine and either allowing the plants to drop to the lake bottom or harvesting them for possible use as fertilizer in farmers' fields. In addition to cost and labor, a drawback of this approach was that "good weeds" were impacted. With no steady source of funds to pay for lake-weed management, the BLPOA made yearly appeals for members to voluntarily donate to a weed fund.

Eventually, it was determined state-approved chemical treatment was the most effective way to manage non-native aquatic weeds. This presented the BLPOA with the major project of raising a sum of money capable of funding a trial chemical control along with its weed-harvesting program. In 1988, the BLPOA decided to only use chemical treatment to manage non-native weeds—a targeted approach, but costly.

Jim McKevitt, BLPOA's president from 2004 to 2005, led the initiative to find solutions for funding and oversight. After much discussion among stakeholders, in 2006 the Summit Township Board (Mason County) put a lake board in place and called it the Bass Lake Improvement Board. The BLIB sets an annual budget for aquatic weed control, contracts with weed assessment and control professionals, and determines required taxation for fulfillment of those responsibilities.

Board membership consists of a lakefront property owner as appointed by the BLPOA, two representatives appointed by the Summit Township Board, a representative of the Mason County Drain Commission, and a Mason County commissioner.

While still challenging, Bass Lake has dedicated eyes on lake-weed management and the funds to put toward it.

Bass Lake For You in '82
(sung to the tune of "Funiculì Funiculà")

Bass Lake, we dearly love to shout your glory,
Up to the sky—Where songbirds fly.
Bass Lake, we proudly share your awesome beauty,
The channel run—The setting sun.
But we, we love to watch bikini skiers!
Away they go—a graceful show.
The air is filled with laughter gaily ringing.
Bask in the sun! Sailing is fun!

Chorus
Fishing, jogging, action everywhere!
Swimming, eating, friends who always share.
Tra-la-la-la, Tra-la-la-la, Tra-la-la-la, Tra-la-la-la,
Happiness is Bass Lake, Tra-la-la-la, Tra-la-la-la!
(Shout) BASS LAKE!

Parody written by Marge Mink for the Bass Lake Property Owners Association's sixty-sixth anniversary party held August 5, 1982, at the Ludington Elks Hall.

Chapter 7

A Storm to Remember

Rain of the Century: 1986

Meteorologists say the 1986 rainstorm was one that occurs only once in one hundred years. It was a locally devastating storm—a four-day, record-setting rain that caused millions of dollars in property damage. It was considered the worst rain ever to hit Mason and Oceana counties, including Bass Lake. The storm began harmlessly enough as a light drizzle on a Tuesday evening. By the time it finally stopped raining two nights later, both counties were operating under a state of emergency.

The weather forecast for Tuesday, September 9, 1986, read accordingly: "Tonight, occasional rain. Wednesday, cloudy, with a 40 percent chance of thunderstorms." By 2:30 a.m. on Wednesday, September 10, the storm had become extremely severe, with thunder, lightning, and strong winds driving heavy rain. By midmorning, washouts and flood conditions were reported on many roads.

A huge chasm just north of the Ludington Pumped Storage Plant on South Lakeshore Drive developed sometime Wednesday morning from the steady pounding of the rain. The impact of the storm was beginning to take shape by midafternoon as more roads were washed out, reports of basement flooding increased, and motorists experienced great difficulty traveling roadways that had become rivers. Bass Lake ran over its banks, damaging cottages and year-round homes in the worst flooding anyone could remember. According to the BLPOA minutes of July 4, 1987:

During the great rains of September 1986, 11.5 inches fell, Bass Lake rose 30 inches, a new channel was formed at the dam, which under washed the foundation on the south side. Loads of dirt were used to plug and fill it. The concrete structure was reinforced and repaired.

"The high water in the fall of 1986 impacted our property, bringing the water level above the seawall and almost to the front steps of the cottage!" wrote Kim Challoner. "My grandfather, Fritz Mink, was able to row a boat in the front yard!"

By Thursday, September 11, the magnitude of the storm was realized. A state of emergency was declared in both Mason and Oceana counties. At 1:00 a.m., US Highway 31 at Kibby Creek was covered with two feet of water. At 7:35 a.m., water behind the Hart Dam on Hart Lake was rising rapidly. Dozens of workers and volunteers frantically engineered sandbags to save the dam. Hart Lake soon took on the appearance of a mud bog rather than a lake. By noon, school was dismissed. As far as anyone can remember, this was the first time school closed for two and a half days due to rain, not snow. By 7:05 p.m., the Hart Dam gave way. The force of the water had literally washed away the bank. A wall of water seven feet high headed toward Pentwater. A red alert was issued for Pentwater as people moved to safer areas.

But as the water neared Pentwater, it diminished in force. When it reached Long Bridge Road at Pentwater Lake, it was barely a foot high. Pentwater escaped without serious problems. By 11:00 p.m., water began to recede, and the threat was over.

Families returned to their homes, and the sun, which hadn't been seen in nearly five days, reappeared. However, numerous roads and bridges would be out for weeks to months.

This "Storm of the Century" occurrence is extremely rare in the Great Lakes area. The band of storms was only three hundred miles in length and fifty to sixty miles wide, but it stalled over western Michigan. Bass Lake and surrounding areas got the worst of it. Incredibly, there was just one report of a minor hospitalization related to the storm. More than 111 storm victims were served at a Red Cross shelter set up at the Mason County Reformed Church in Scottville. Approximately three hundred hours were logged by Red Cross volunteers and staff at the center, and its services were needed for twenty-two days after the storm.

Chapter 8
Boating and Fishing on Bass Lake

Bass Lake Property Owners Association members look forward to their annual spring newsletter providing need-to-know info about what's happened at Bass Lake over the winter and what's going to happen in the summer.

In the 1973 newsletter, BLPOA President Karl H. Jepson reported that ice fishing was good, and that many tiger muskies were caught:

Some were too small to keep, but some were 30-inches to 35-inches and should be ready for summer. The ice went out of the lake about March 7, a month earlier than usual. The Bass Lake water level is the highest in my memory. It has been difficult to open the channel into Lake Michigan and keep it open. At one time, the water must have been 20-inches to 24-inches above the dam. On April 1, with water running into Lake Michigan, the water depth over the dam was 12-inches. All this has done considerable damage to waterfront property and seawalls. Lake Michigan is nearly at its second all-time high and is a big contributor to our high-water problems.

All of this was important and spoke to prospects for the upcoming vacation, boating, and fishing season at Bass Lake.

Early Days: Fishing

As early real estate developers enticed people to visit Bass Lake, the opportunity to bathe, boat, and fish on a peaceful, sandy-bottomed lake connected to Lake Michigan was a huge draw. Good fishing was especially important as folks oftentimes relied on the day's catch for meals.

An exuberant John E. Ramsey was happy to be at Bass Lake circa 1940.

In the early 1900s, the Wayt's Hotel advertised that Bass Lake was well supplied with bass, pickerel, pike, and all kinds of small fish: "Two trout streams run into the lake. Other good fishing lakes and streams are nearby. The lake is a beautiful sheet of water and offers exceptional advantages for fishing and boating."

In 1973, a Smert's Resort leaflet optimistically opined:

If you like to fish, you won't go home empty-handed. Some fish that can be caught are Tiger Muskie, Northern Pike, Bass, Blue Gills, Crappie, Bullheads. Many nice Bass, Pike or Muskie are caught right off one of our piers! As far as panfish, you can catch as many as your family feels like cleaning (the limit of course)!

The resort's leaflet sported fish graphics and a photo with a large catch strung on a fishing line. It also claimed that you would find the fish have a sweeter flavor out of Bass Lake due to all the artesian (flowing) wells along the lake's east side.

Over the years, one of the things the BLPOA worked to improve was recreational fishing in Bass Lake. Partnering with the Michigan State

Wanzer family

Fish were bountiful in the early 1900s. Bass, blue gill, northern pike, pickerel, tiger muskie, and more swam in Bass Lake waters. The Bass Lake Park Improvement Association assigned a committee to look after stocking the lake to keep anglers happy.

University fisheries, at times the lake was stocked with game fish such as tiger muskie, northern pike, muskellunge, and walleye. Unfortunately, walleye fishing was not very successful due to the shallow nature of Bass Lake. In 1966, Michigan's Department of Natural Resources took over the regulation of fish stocking programs. By 1970, the permitting process and associated costs made stocking the lake with approved fish nearly impossible.

For many years, there was a weeklong Pike Festival on Bass Lake. Mary Thiele remembered that "there wasn't a regular date; it just depended on how thick the ice was. Cars with shanties—and even without— would drive on the ice to form a large circle. There were even motorcycles, snowmobiles, and bicycles. That week there were many happy fishermen due to the comradeship and the abundance of their chosen beverages. Even a food trailer showed up to feed the festivalgoers." Unfortunately, the festival ended in the early 2000s due to significant post-festival cleanup and trash left behind on the ice.

After the last Pike Festival, Mary recalled that winters were colder, making it difficult to stay outside for long. "My husband, Hank, would drill his fishing hole in the ice in front of the house. After placing his tip-ups, he'd hurry back to the house to watch from the window!"

Ice fishing continues to evolve on the lake. Today's generation of die-hard Bass Lake ice fishermen prep for comfort by

Thiele family

Henry Fred Thiele, an avid fisherman, showed off his catch while ice fishing on Bass Lake in 1938.

equipping themselves with large tents, heaters, TVs, cell phones, and cooking stoves.

Bortell's: West Michigan's Fish Fry

Bass Lakers eventually discover Bortell's Fisheries, an off-the-beaten-track culinary gem about two miles north of the lake on South Lakeshore Drive. A square, brightly painted cinder block building with a fish-shaped sign is where locals and vacationers find what's arguably the most delicious fresh fish in West Michigan.

Since 1898 and six generations later, the Bortell family still serves up their smoked and fried fish. Decades ago, they used to operate a fishing boat from Bortell's Landing, located on Lake Michigan across the road from the restaurant. The Bortell family generously donated some of the land in 1926 to Summit Township for a public park and swimming beach. Their fishing operations ceased when the Michigan Department of Natural Resources ended commercial fishing on Lake Michigan in 1973. Now, Bortell's fish is typically sourced from Alaska and Canada.

The Old Family Recipe

Current owner Kris Bortell shared the family's secrets of success.

"For six generations our family has advertised old-fashioned wood-smoked fish. We smoke fish without chemicals or gas, use electric heat to hurry the smoking process, and rely on only wood for fire—and experience—to consistently produce quality wood-smoked fish. The sad thing is a person with an outdoor grill could technically claim the same thing. But without 120 years of experience, there are details that are likely to be neglected or even unknown."

—Kris Bortell

From Oars to Motors

In the early days, if traveling from Pentwater to Bass Lake via Lake Michigan, rowboats were essential to maneuver over sandbars into the calm waters of the Outlet. In addition to transportation, rowboats and canoes dotted Bass Lake for all kinds of recreational use.

Just as it is today, boating was a big part of everyday fun for Bass Lake children. When Betty Gilbert Ligon and her brother, Robert, went turtle hunting, one would row gently toward a log with sunning turtles on it, while the other crouched in the bow, ready to grab. Sometimes they would catch one and take it home to keep in one of the round laundry tubs. "No matter what we did to secure it, the turtle was gone in the morning. Mother denied any knowledge of their escapes," she said. Betty also described water fights with friends. "Bob Gannett, Ed Tweedie, and I in one rowboat, and Robert, Sonny Gannett, and maybe Doug Tweedie in another—we used the oars to splash each other. We were drenched. Mother never scolded, [she] just got out dry clothes."

Wind and waves were always factors to be considered when one rowed on Lake Michigan. Robert Gilbert sheepishly recalled such a day when conditions became challenging. "My good friend Steve Johnson and I rowed to Bortell's Landing in the late morning with the provisions while Mother and her sister-in-law, Julia Gilbert, walked along the beach." After enjoying a lunch of fried chicken, sandwiches, and pie, it was time to return. "The wind had freshened from the southwest and the waves were building," continued Robert. "The humiliation of Steve and myself, on being told that Mother and Julia would therefore row back, was complete. I shall never forget looking out beyond the breakers to see those fiftyish ladies sturdily rowing in unison against the wind and waves. I've forgotten whether they beat us to the Outlet or not. Probably they did."

Many Bass Lake stories include accounts of oarsmen tackling the Outlet channel while confronting precariously perched logs and hidden stumps, resulting in nature's obstacle course. Olga Doty recounted, "We rowed down the Outlet to the beach, winding in and out amongst beautiful pines. The Outlet resembled a small waterfall, where children dived and swam. Upon arrival we found this beautiful beach, which was breathtaking after our crowded beaches in Chicago."

Eventually, oars were replaced with motors—a time-saving miracle! The first Evinrude outboard motors were introduced in 1909. These motors were easily attached to the backs of rowboats, deck boats, and other vessels to help their drivers navigate the waters more quickly and expertly as

By the 1930s, small motors were being added to rowboats.

they went about their tasks—fishing, hauling trees, transporting cargo, and more. In the 1920s, the first wooden boats used only for recreational purposes—also known as runabouts—were introduced. They were originally small, fast, powerful, varnished wooden boats created to take advantage of the power of outboard motors.

"As a child, I was happiest when we took the steel boat steered by my father and propelled by the blue, 3-horsepower Johnson motor to Lake Michigan," wrote Charlotte Gilbert Drayer. "We'd sing over the noise of the motor all the way to the weir."

Debbie Wlodarski remembered many rowboats from the 1960s. A few, if you were lucky, had a small outboard motor—some were 3–8 hp. Soon, boats at Bass Lake got faster.

Speedboats Arrive: Life in the Fast Lane

Hank Thiele's childhood featured a legendary collection of boats. His dad stacked two powerboats on a trailer and brought them to Michigan each summer. When he was only six, Hank got his first motor, an Evinrude 5-hp. At age twelve, weighing about one hundred pounds, Hank skied behind an aluminum rowboat with a 9-hp motor. It could reach speeds of 24 mph.

Bass Lake water-skier Valentin Krecko enjoyed an early morning run with his brother-in-law, Dan Patsos, at the helm. This unique backdrop is the Ludington Pumped Storage Project to the north of Bass Lake.

He still has his great-grandfather's 16-hp motor, which weighs about 150 pounds. Folks used metal-can floats on the back of each boat to keep the weight of the motor from sinking the boat in the rear. Powerboat racing was a popular weekend activity. Hank said, "Boats could reach upwards of 55 mph with those old motors. The fishermen didn't like the boats racing, but the motors aerated the water, and the fish would start biting."

Faster boats brought water sports like waterskiing to Bass Lake. In the 1950s, a ski jump existed toward the lake's north end. Dick Warner's family built a 1950s cabin near Schlick's Resort. Dick was a competitive swimmer and needed to practice his turns. Thus, his dad built him a swimmer's turnaround in the lake and a ski jump.

Waterskiing and pleasure boating became popular on Bass Lake. Kim Challoner learned to ski at the age of nine. Once she could ski, there was no stopping her in regard to water sports. Her mother, Vicki Poplstein, often commented that if Kim could have read a book while driving the boat, she could have read an entire library! Kim's love for Bass Lake and water sports was passed on to her daughters, Jackie and Katie, who learned to ski by age five and later took their skills to their university's waterskiing team. Kim said, "Our family is always looking for the calm water to ski."

Randy Holmes recalled daily adventures at the Outlet as a young boy. "It was always a treat when the older kids would give us boat rides. The Shaw family had a light blue hydroplane—a small boat with an outboard motor that was low to the water and felt exciting to just simply sit in. Really made me feel special." The Hillman family was also into hydroplanes. According to Harry Hillman IV, his grandfather, Harry Hillman II, liked to race Class C hydroplanes.

It's clear Bass Lakers enjoy lake time in many ways—waterskiing, wakeboarding, tubing, swimming, fishing, rowing, sailing, kayaking, canoeing, paddleboarding, or just lounging on a pontoon boat and viewing the sunset. In any case, it's just a typical day on the lake.

Chapter 9
Smooth Sailing

For two weeks every summer, lucky Bass Lake visitors can enjoy a welcome sight from their docks: fleets of sailboats gliding majestically across shimmering blue water in the annual Bass Lake Sailing Club races. But the history of sailboat racing on the lake actually goes back to the beginning of the 20th century, when rowboats were powered by opened umbrellas and home-sewn sails and steered by jerry-rigged rudders. These makeshift vessels gave way to wooden sailboats and eventually sleek fiberglass, class-legal sailboats. The spirit of fun and competition of both these pickup and organized races has remained consistent over the decades.

The Bass Lake Sailing Club was started in 1962 when Dick Kraybill, a Kodak chemical engineer, got together with five of his friends for informal sailing races that were then scored on a handicap system to determine the winner. Included in the group were Kraybill, on his Day Sailer, Ondine; John Gilbert with his Whistler; Bob Masten, who sailed a Snipe; Frank Pielsticker with a Penguin; and a Sunfish belonging to Lou Mooney. Dick Kraybill loved to sail, and he wanted to teach sailing and encourage others to participate in the sport. The season consists of twelve races and culminates with an award ceremony with ribbons and trophies awarded to the top-finishing participants in each fleet.

The Bass Lake Sailing Club

For over sixty years, the Bass Lake Sailing Club (BLSC) has welcomed area sailors to participate in annual sailing races on the lake. In 2021, Wendy Jonkers, commodore of the BLSC, shared an invitation for both novices

Stanley Wanzer at the helm of his pride and joy, a wooden Crescent sailboat circa 1940. The boat is still stored in the Wanzer family's Bass Lake boathouse.

Sails dot the shoreline before the start of the first Bass Lake Sailing Club race. Commodore John Finch makes announcements from the committee dock circa 1980.

and seasoned sailors to join in on the fun. In the "Welcome to Pentwater" introduction in the August edition of the *Pentwater This Week* magazine that year, Wendy shared a little more about the club:

> For two incredibly special weeks each summer, Bass Lake comes alive with colorful sails. Skippers navigate to the southwest corner of the lake for the start of the Bass Lake Sailing Club races, just as they have done for almost 60 years. As long as there have been sailboats on Bass Lake, there has been friendly competition between sailors. In the early 1960s, a group of family and friends decided to formalize the competition and organize races for sailboats, complete with markers on a designated course, a starting horn, a volunteer dock committee, trophies, and bragging rights.
>
> In the early days of the races, many different types of sailboats competed, and a handicap number was assigned to each boat to determine the winner after the calculations were done. My father (Stan Wanzer) was one of the earliest sailors with the Club, and he

sailed an old wooden Crescent. The popularity of Sunfish sailboats in the 1970s meant that another fleet was formed, which happens any time there are at least three of the same type of boats sailing in a race. In addition to the Handicap and Sunfish fleets, we now also have a Laser fleet.

To encourage greater participation, each sailboat was required to have crew, the lighter the better, so kids were always chosen first. Those same kids who started out as crew, moved on to skipper their own boats, recruited their children as crew, and are now proudly watching their grandchildren participate in the Bass Lake Sailing Club races each summer. When folks get that Pentwater sand between their toes, they keep coming back, summer after summer, generation after generation, just as the Bass Lake sailors keep coming back to race again.

Charity Monroe

Boats in the Bass Lake Sailing Club's 2019 handicap fleet are anxious to be the first to cross the start line at the sound of the horn. Some of these same sailboats participated in the 1962 inaugural season of the BLSC and have participated in the fleet ever since.

Forty Years of Fair Winds and Following Seas

Ginny Kraybill Patsos, daughter of Bass Lake Sailing Club founder Dick Kraybill, shared these remarks at the club's 40th anniversary celebration in August 2002:

I remember my dad was tuned in, sharp and intent on making the Day Sailer go just as fast as he could. My dad won many awards, but he made the crew feel like we were the ones who did a lot of the winning. It was always fun sailing with Dad.

I recall Frank Blymyer sailing his sailing canoe and doing a beautiful job. John Gilbert's Flying Dutchman was the big boat in the old days. The Crosses' Osprey was always a contender in heavy winds. Fred Williams in his Jetwind, Karl Jepson in his Sunfish, Ron Hamelen in a Snipe, and Sandy and Don Pippert in an M-16 scow that was always capsizing. The beautiful Friendship 13 was patiently sailed by Martie Finch.

The Butterflies were another class. Norm Halverson, Howard and son John Decker, Bob Beckman Sr. and Jr., Lester Baker, Charlie Barrow, and later Dan Patsos, to name a few. The Sunfish had many champions: Steve and Tombo Erley, Mary Green, David Cross, Will Wright, and Charlotte, Charity, and Hank Gilbert. We have kept the Sunfish fleet strong for a long time.

One of my favorite memories was cutting out pennants, also known as the Pennant Party. My mom (Jean) would scour the area for blue, red, and green cotton cloth. We would all get together at the No-wiki-wiki cottage to trace, cut out, and label pennants just prior to the Awards Day ceremony. Someone was usually playing a guitar—Bennett Cross was the best. One year, Lester Baker, a thirteen-year-old crew member, drank twelve orange soda pops at the party—and lived to sail on!

There have been some fun traditions: Boat parades at the tenth and twenty-fifth anniversaries. We used to play sailboat tag a lot—the teenagers mostly. Alyssa Roberts and Macy Allen purposely capsized a Sunfish one hundred times, but who's counting? With Linda Jepson, we capsized just after the race ended. With Kevin Mooney, we casually sailed backwards into the weeds. A funny thing now, but it seemed disastrous at the time, was the docks floating away when the water got too high in the late seventies and collapsed again in 2001!

Being on the dock was a whole different story. The Dock Committee had to have octopuses' capabilities to sight, time, record, announce, *raise flags, take dues, settle controversies, cancel races, and endure driving rains and floods. Clocks failed, watches got water in them, skippers mysteriously jumped ship or traded crew. Some of the long serving dock crew were Jean Kraybill, Kitty Williams, Sandy Cross, Madeline Hamelen, Marian Cerny, and Grace Holland. We have been graced by the Cerny family, who were so active in getting a "B" fleet started and training the troops. You name it, they have all helped keep this club going, as do all the present members. The club has great strength along with the spirit of good friendship and good sailing.*

Charity Monroe

John Decker was part of the Bass Lake community his whole life. Since the 1960s, he and his Butterfly sailboat Sweetie had sailed with the BLSC. Sadly, John passed away while boating on Bass Lake on July 23, 2021. John's wife, Betsy, shared that "Bass Lake was John's favorite place on earth, and he died doing what he loved best." John was a friend to many and always ready with a joke, story, or a helping hand. In 2022, his lifelong friend, Pete Olsen, established the Bass Lake Sailing Club's "John Decker Memorial Sportsmanship Award" to honor one of our own.

Chapter 10
The Ever-Changing Landscape

Many Bass Lakers claim the best part of arriving at the lake is taking in their first view of the shimmering water nestled in a lush, green landscape—a view that never changes. The reality, of course, is that weather, modernization, changing roads, nature, and innovation have always played a role in altering the Bass Lake area's landscape.

Armistice Day, 1940: Struggle to Keep the Outlet Open

The November 11, 1940, Armistice Day storm was one of the worst in Lake Michigan recorded history. Two freighters were lost between Little Point Sable and Big Point Sable—*William B. Davock* and *Anna C. Minch*. The ships foundered. None of the crew survived. Another ship—*Novadoc*—was driven aground south of Pentwater. In icy winds and freezing water, a boat of local fishermen bravely rescued the *Novadoc* crew. Bass Lake resident Clara Parbs wrote letters chronicling the storm's effect on the Bass Lake Outlet and surrounding area. In one letter she recorded the storm's path of destruction:

> *The sand is solid up to the top of the dam. Straight across the whole opening filled in as though water never flowed there. [The area east] of the dam Payton Copas says is filled with oats off the boat that was wrecked. God only knows what we will find when we dig it out. The dam seems safe enough from what I saw, and the rickety bridge is still there, but I did not try it.*
>
> *Perhaps if they could get a team in to drag? You remember how hard we worked to keep the Outlet open in the summer. THIS can never break through, 5 feet deep it is. Not without help. If we have*

no Outlet, we cannot take care of all the water that empties into Bass Lake. The water there will stagnate, and it will again be a mosquito nest, as it was before my time. Or has the time come when our beautiful Outlet is to be another gully between the dunes to Lake Michigan—and simply dry?

Clara wrote a second appeal to get the Outlet water flowing again:

Yesterday I talked to Mrs. Schlick, and she said something must be done to lower the level of the lake, or we will all be under. She had also spoken with a man who predicted if the Outlet was not again opened—that Bass Lake will rise 8 feet this winter. Mrs. Schlick is worried. Those having basements will be flooded. Morrisons' lakefront cottages are in danger. There will be no Outlet.

Clara goes on to suggest hiring a crew of four or five men for several days, perhaps longer, at three dollars per day so the Outlet can be opened:

The weather is fine, and it could be done. Because the boards are out, thank goodness it gave the sand a place to go and did not knock out the dam with the pressure upon it from the Lake Michigan side. This must all be done before it freezes.

After much effort, the Outlet was successfully reopened.

Teapot Dome: From Gas Station to Apartments

To some, the term "Teapot Dome" refers to the 1920s Washington, DC, scandal during President Warren Harding's administration. At that time, the secretary of the U.S. Department of the Interior secretly leased government oil fields to private companies in exchange for bribes. One of these oil fields was known as Teapot Dome. What does that have to do with Bass Lake? Bass Lake had a Teapot Dome, but it wasn't exactly an oil field.

This Teapot Dome was a Sinclair gas service station and a small two-story store. It was located on US Highway 31 north of Pentwater and very close to Bass Lake. With more and more automobiles and summer vacationers traveling through Oceana and Mason counties, around 1927 John Grondsma ran a popular, growing business. His wife and many children also called the Teapot Dome home.

Due to easy access to US-31, the service station was a popular place to shop and served as a drop-off / pickup point for those traveling to Camp Morrison and other Bass Lake destinations. When John passed away in 1952, the property and business were sold. After 2007, it was repurposed as the Main Event Restaurant and apartments. Today, only apartments remain. But the astute eye can still imagine the Teapot Dome's early beginnings.

Dick Ouweneel

One of the few early businesses near Bass Lake, the Teapot Dome gasoline station and store on Business US Highway 31 provided valued services to the community. Many of the structures seen in this circa 1940s photo still exist; however, they're used for different purposes.

US Highway 31 Extension: Differing Opinions

In the early days, roads ran where they were convenient and not necessarily where they were platted. The roads looked different back then compared with today—Thiele Road was a dead end and didn't go all the way to the Outlet; Mack Road didn't even exist. The condition of local roads became much more important when foot traffic on these thoroughfares decreased, and automobile traffic increased. South Lakeshore Drive used to be a two-track, and now cars whizz by.

Many old-timers reminisce about their first car ride to the summer cottage. Just when Bass Lake seemed in sight, the freeway narrowed to the rutted one-lane Pere Marquette Highway, which meandered through tiny towns like Niles and New Era. In the early 1970s, the interstate highway system began to extend its way up western Michigan. First was the creation of I-96 / US Highway 31 in Berrien County, and two years later, the northern US Highway 31 was extended into Oceana County. The following year, the highway was completed, ending at the intersection with US Highway 10 at Ludington.

Two routes were proposed for the US Highway 31 extension from Oceana County into Mason County—one close to the east side of Bass Lake, and another further east through farmlands. At an April 1973 meeting of the Mason County Planning Commission, representatives from the BLPOA argued that the route closest to Bass Lake would cause severe ecological problems, would uproot too many families, and would be a general nuisance to residents. In 1974, a compromise alternative route was proposed, running between the two original ones. BLPOA members went to Lansing several times to meet with representatives of the Michigan Department of State Highways. Their efforts were successful, and by fall 1974, the state highway commission approved a route further from Bass Lake.

The reaction to "New 31" was mixed. There was great enthusiasm for a faster, more convenient route. However, there was some consternation that when the wind was just right, the noisy eighteen-wheelers could be heard lumbering up the new road, interrupting the peaceful lake landscape.

Dealing With Weeds: A Necessary Nuisance

Bass Lake Park Improvement Association (BLPIA) meeting records show aquatic vegetation (a.k.a. lake weeds) has been a concern for decades. In the early 1900s, the BLPIA likely only dealt with native plants that were typical for Michigan lakes. The plants grew to maturity, then died off.

In 1928, the BLPIA spent $670 on a weed-cutting machine to clear paths across the lake so boats could traverse more easily. This mechanical "technology" was a skiff fitted with a Model T engine. It was fondly named "Pluto" and had a sickle bar that was lowered into the water about four feet to cut the lake weeds. Cut weeds simply floated on the surface, washed on shore, or sank to the bottom.

Here comes Pluto! Shown in 1941, this weed-cutting machine was used for decades to manage aquatic plants growing in Bass Lake. It's believed Payton Copas, a back-in-the-day cottage caretaker, is at Pluto's helm.

Many Bass Lake residents took turns operating and repairing Pluto. Local youth were paid ten cents an hour to run the machine, whereas professionals (adults) were paid twenty-five cents an hour. Some of those who ran Pluto included Ted Chapman, Stan Wanzer, and Payton Copas, a trusted Bass Lake caretaker. Laude Hartrum II, who was a teenager when Pluto was decommissioned, retained the privilege of being Pluto's last standing captain. The mechanical weed-harvesting approach continued for decades.

Eventually, in the mid-1960s, Michigan lakes saw the arrival of an invasive, non-native species called curly-leaf pondweed. This prolific plant grows early in the spring, creating a dense mat that inhibits native aquatic plants. Thanks to sufficient monetary donations, the Bass Lake Property Owners Association (formerly the BLPIA) continued its efforts to control the weeds.

In 1971, Pluto was retired, and Norman E. Maney's Aquatic Services took over. He engineered a weed-cutter that resembled a barge with submerged cutter bars in front and on the sides. It had an underwater weed-catcher elevator to dump the cut weeds on the surface of the barge. This mechanical approach was somewhat successful for the time.

Then a second invasive non-native weed, called Eurasian watermilfoil, showed up in Bass Lake. It was found that chemical treatment is the most effective way to control this aggressive, well-established plant. The BLPOA decided to stop using mechanical means to manage weeds and to use chemicals instead. But chemical treatment is very costly. It became clear that funding through BLPOA donations could not keep up. In 2003, the BLPOA spent thirty thousand dollars on chemical weed control, but a comprehensive weed control plan was expected to cost fifty thousand dollars. A solution as to how to fairly fund this cost was pursued under the leadership of Jim McKevitt, a longtime Bass Lake resident and BLPOA president.

In 2006, the Summit Township Board (Mason County) formed the Bass Lake Improvement Board (BLIB) to manage aquatic weeds. This approach ensures necessary funds are available to cover the expense of an aquatic engineer, a qualified chemical applicator, and Michigan-approved chemicals. Because some of these aquatic invasive plants are so prolific and cannot be eradicated, the ongoing goal is to manage the bad ones and encourage the growth of good native species—always striving for a balanced aquatic landscape.

Willis Wright

Could this be the old weed-cutter Pluto circa 1998? Described by Willis Wright as a "familiar hulk," it was for sale at the corner of Hancock and Lowell streets in Pentwater. Memories live on, but nothing lasts forever.

The Project: Energy in the Bluffs

A marvel to behold from a boat on Lake Michigan, the Ludington Pumped Storage Plant sits on a thousand-acre site along the lake's shoreline, four miles south of Ludington. Started in 1969, it required roughly four years to complete and was dubbed "The Project" by Bass Lake and Ludington locals. It forever changed the landscape north of Bass Lake.

At the time of its completion in 1973, the Ludington Pumped Storage Plant was the largest of its kind in the world. Today, co-owned by Consumers Energy and DTE Electric, it's an important component in their plan to lower carbon emissions and provide a reliable supply of electricity.

The Ludington Pumped Storage Plant takes advantage of the natural, steep sand-dune formation of eastern Lake Michigan. Its asphalt-and-clay reservoir is a large, man-made, 842-acre lake atop a bluff. Water is pumped from a lower reservoir—in this case, Lake Michigan—to the upper reservoir, then released downhill through supersized turbines to create electricity.

Essentially, it's a hydroelectric power plant used during times of peak power demand. The Ludington Pumped Storage Plant could be described as one of the world's largest batteries because it holds vast amounts of potential energy ready to power the electric grid for 1.4 million households.

Wind Energy: Powering the Future

In 2012, a new kind of farm came to Mason County in the form of the Lake Winds Energy Park. A wind farm of fifty-six turbines, it's operated by Consumers Energy and can provide one hundred megawatts of electricity.

The Lake Winds Energy Park changed the landscape of Bass Lake. Dozens of turbines situated on agricultural land north and east of the lake are easily visible from many docks. Up close, the five-hundred-foot-tall structures loom large. One local resident reflected on the reaction of many to the twirling newcomers, saying that the sight took some getting used to, but the more they looked at them, the more graceful they became.

The Lake Winds Energy Park, along with the nearby Pumped Storage Plant, put Mason County at the forefront of clean, renewable energy for all of Michigan.

Many of the fifty-six Lake Winds Energy Park turbines can be seen above the treetops at Bass Lake.

PART 2

Chapter 11
Bass Lake Adventures

Each person who has ever been to Bass Lake in the summer has a Bass Lake history, complete with special memories and favorite things to do. What better way to capture the essence of Bass Lake and all of the enchantment it holds than to let some longtime Bass Lakers share their family experiences and what makes Bass Lake special to them.

Randy Holmes

Sit here a while and take in this beautiful Bass Lake day—the warm sun, the incredibly blue sky, and the breeze stirring softly in the trees. Contemporary Bass Lakers share their stories and why they find Bass Lake so endearing.

My Story: A Tale of Two Lakes
—Carla Barrow

The newsletter excerpt which opens this book is truly a gem. It was discovered tucked away in the original *Bass Lake Property Owners Scrapbook* on a faint mimeographed sheet of paper. My favorite line is the last one: "[The water] flows past the home of the fairies, tumbles over the dam, and scampers across the beach to the welcoming arms of the Big Lake." This sentence perfectly describes our cherished Outlet—nestled in the land of Bass Lake Enchantment.

On Bass Lake, docks and piers become extensions of our cottages that are accessible to us in mere minutes. We can effortlessly zip around on a motorboat or enjoy a more leisurely pace in a kayak, canoe, or pontoon. The experience of sailing on Bass Lake is at the heart of so many stories accompanied by several articles describing the Bass Lake Sailing Club throughout the years. There is much our small lake has to offer.

What becomes so delightful is the transition from the trimmed-down little lake as you begin your journey to the majestic big lake. Your first point of reference is the lily pads—and you must slow down because there are just so many, and it's stunning and delightful to see them showing off in their summertime glory. Your next point of reference is the sign stating "No Wake Zone" ahead. The whole tempo changes and you immediately shift gears to weave through the continuously bending waterway while viewing the serene wildlife.

But soon you hear Lake Michigan rumble and realize something bigger is coming your way. No wonder the Little Lake is getting pumped to hang out with the Big Lake. When they converge, the magic is sealed with this merger of two lakes, embracing one another. For us, arriving at the top of the dune and catching a glimpse of the precious Outlet below is a moment of great comfort and gratitude. Now you race down to greet this fantastic beach and enjoy all that it generously offers.

We recall the familiar ritual of family members, shovels in hand, heading for the Outlet to help "dig it out." Bass Lakers take great pride in and ownership of their beloved Outlet, and throughout its history how to best maintain the Outlet and take good care of it continues to be an ongoing discussion. How fortunate we are to have these two lakes.

My Story: Bass Lake Fondest Memories
—Kyle Gilbert Chapman

While my family history around Bass Lake started in 1895, most everything between then and 1960 is from stories told around the table, lake, or beach. We had four family units, and we all shared three cottages. OK, two cottages and one very small log home. As most of my aunts and uncles were teachers, they all wanted to spend as much time as possible at the lake.

Being the next to the youngest of six children, and since my little sister and I didn't take up too much sleeping space, we were frequently "farmed out" to one of the other cottages and moved several times over the summer. The big advantage to this was knowing what was for dinner, and if we didn't like it, we had a good excuse to see if there were better options.

Our grandmother, Neva Gilbert Chapman, chose to stay with our family. Never did know why but I think it had something to do with my mother's cooking. As our family grew, with older siblings getting married and having kids, it became more difficult to have us all in one place as so many were arriving at different times. So our family was the chosen one to move every couple of weeks and occasionally rent area cottages from the Ronnebergs, the Hillmans, or the Collinses. The things that never changed, though, were the weekly all-family meals at the 1920s cottage and the evening card games at the log cabin built by my great-grandfather.

As we got older, like so many kids up here, our rules were pretty loose and would never pass today's muster. We would head out in the morning to find our friends around the lake. Sometimes by rowboat, occasionally by sailboat, but most often on foot or bicycle. Lunch could be at anyone's cottage and usually consisted of a peanut butter sandwich with potato chips crushed on it (at Steve Baker's), or a peanut butter and jelly sandwich with Cheetos and carrots (at Todd Decker's), or whatever we had last night at our place. If we didn't check in by dinner time, our curfew was a little after dark. With a check-in, midnight was almost always okay.

Our best family gathering was in 1975, with over thirty of us. This was my time to put the time-honored Bass Lake trial to the test. The standing rule in our family was, "If you bring a potential spouse up to the lake with all the family present and they don't like being there, it wasn't meant to be." Pam passed the test with flying colors. At one point my sister Lynne came up to me and whispered, "This is the one; now don't blow it." We just celebrated our forty-eighth anniversary!

Our Story: Summer Freedom and Reforestation
—Willis and Nancy Wright

Now in his ninth decade, Willis recalls his earliest memories of Bass Lake from when he was not much more than an infant. Shelton Wright, Willis's father, and George Finch were veterans of World War I, and they both worked for Belden Wire Corporation, George in Chicago and Shelton in Detroit. After George extolled the virtues of a summer at Bass Lake, his co-worker Shelton decided to rent the Bird House from the Finch family so that his family could spend the summer at Bass Lake, which they did for many years. Shelton was a traveling salesman and would come back to the lake every week or two, while his mother, Jean, and Willis's brother, Newell, and sister, Carolyn, spent halcyon days at the lake.

Willis's earliest memories of the Bird House were of the water pump, outhouse, and path to the lake. He'd walk out the door in the morning, dodging the chores that needed to be done, and be gone the whole morning. Willis knew where all the trails were and hiked to Baldy and then out to the beach. He'd get around in a rowboat. Life was carefree, and no one cared where he went, and no one bothered him or hounded him about wearing a life jacket. Willis's idea of fun was to go to the Outlet and catch turtles. On one adventure in the Outlet, he managed to get a snapping turtle in the rowboat and was scared for his life. The whole Wright family would go to the square dances at Camp Morrison, and Willis still remembers the calls.

F.E. Pray, the developer of the plot in which the Wrights own property, had tried to market the land to people in the South, promising them cool summers in the woods and on the shores of Bass Lake. Pray had to do quite a bit of work to bundle together the properties as there were many anonymous lots in the tract. After doing title searches, Pray had to obtain a letter stating that the owners had no interest and could transfer the properties via quitclaim deed, of which there are dozens.

Eventually the Wrights acquired forty acres, and then another twenty-two, and owned up to the base of Fairview. The adjoining forty acres facing the beach and including the dunes were available, and Shelton Wright could have purchased the property for one hundred dollars an acre but didn't have the resources at the time. The cottage was cramped, so Shelton hired a carpenter and built a forty-foot screened porch, a kitchen, and a dining room extension. The Wright family has lost count of all of the dozens of friends and family who visited them at the lake and piled in to sleep on that big porch.

Shelton would carry pipes into the woods to mark the corners of the properties, and Willis would etch a "W" into those cement markers. Those concrete markers continue to do the job today nearly a century later, defining the corners of the Wright property.

Slowly but steadily, Shelton was acquiring free state-supplied trees, which were mostly spruces and red pine. These small seedlings were delivered to the cottage, usually right outside the back door, in a box of five thousand at a time. The family was instructed that every time they went into the woods, they should take a tree and plant it in a bare spot, so the whole family would grab shovels and buckets full of seedlings, go back behind the cottage, and start filling in bare spots with the young trees. Shelton often made solo runs with buckets of trees. Willis's perspective at the time was that they were doing menial labor, but now he is quite proud of what they accomplished, filling in the sand blows and areas where the old oil wells were. To this day, if you see a spruce or red pine in the woods, chances are it was probably planted.

"A half hour by the shore of Bass Lake is therapy." —Willis Wright

The Finch family had a Crescent sailboat, which the Wright family developed a great fondness for. In his business travels, Shelton found another Crescent, bought it, and then they had a boat in need of work. Willis's mother, Jean Wright, made a sail for it, even though she had no previous sailmaking abilities, and it was good to go. Now Willis had a boat he could sail.

Enter the Sunfish sailboat, which very quickly appeared on the scene and became very popular with young sailors in the late 1960s and early 1970s. Shelton showed up with one, and it quickly folded into the fleet. The Sunfish was an immediate hit and was in continuous use. The Wrights added more Sunfish to the family fleet and were active participants in the Bass Lake Sailing Club each season. Even now, if you look out at Bass Lake, you'll probably see a Wright sailing a Sunfish.

Years later Willis brought his future bride, Nancy, to Bass Lake for the first time, and Nancy remembers her inaugural sailing venture with Willis on the Crescent. The pair were coming into dock much too fast. Nancy was at the helm, and Willis yelled, "Into the wind!" Suddenly, one of those infamous Bass Lake gusts on the western shore caught the sail, and the boat quickly capsized. This early baptism in Bass Lake never deterred Nancy from enjoying many years of sailing on Bass Lake and sharing her love of sailing with their three sons. After fifty years of marriage and just as many Bass Lake summers together, Willis and Nancy could still be seen on a calm afternoon on Bass Lake, sailing side by side in Sunfish sailboats.

My Story: Expeditions and Adventures
—Dennis J. Dooley

Our grandparents often shared stories about some of the many special events which they looked forward to all year. This included attending a square dance at Camp Morrison, from which the twinkling lights and sounds could be seen and heard all the way from the other side of Bass Lake.

In my day, there were vast games of Capture the Flag that stretched over the dunes; ball games at Summit Park; and battling the huge breakers that sometimes rolled, churning their foam as they drove on the Lake Michigan shore.

But the most anticipated event of each summer was a challenge we confronted in the cold light of day. On the appointed day we would strike out into the woods just south of the Outlet with as many of our McKevitt, Rischar, and McMullin cousins as could be rounded up—for an expedition to the summit of the storied Eagle Top. The steep, sandy climb (the densely pine-covered Eagle Top is actually a gigantic dune) was surely as taxing as the ascent of Mt. Everest and, what's more, involved dodging poison ivy and the occasional timber rattler. The reward was to run head over heels down the sandy dune that deposited us laughing and screaming at the foot of Lake Michigan.

Some summers, if we were up for an even bigger challenge, we would mount an expedition comprising the whole linked series of giant, forested dunes that began with Eagle Top and moved south along the Michigan shore with Castle Mound, Blueberry Ridge, Baldy, and the double-crested Camel's Back. On the far side of Eagle Top was a mysterious clearing where the summer breeze ruffled a blanket of ferns. According to Bobby Rischar, it was an ancient Native American burial ground, and we always maintained a reverent distance as we proceeded to Blueberry Ridge.

Other traditions developed. The younger folk began hanging out at the Hungry Dragon or the ice cream parlor in Pentwater, where double scoops of the legendary Blue Moon became the order of the day—while the older generations browsed the knickknacks that crammed the aisles of Gustafson's and Lite's Drugstore. And of course, there continued to be many quick trips to the Wishing Well, where you could even make a wish if you wanted to.

Our Story: The Bass Lake Discovery
—The Cerny family

Traverse City was the 1974 Cerny vacation destination. Marian, Bill, and their four daughters (Elaine, eighteen; Jean, seventeen; Mary, fourteen; and Carol, eleven) were looking forward to the annual camping trip. The family had moved from Rochester, New York, to South Bend, Indiana, in 1972. It became obvious in the summer of 1973 that going from Indiana to camp in upstate New York was too far to continue spending vacations there. Bill suggested exploring Michigan for the summer.

But two events occurred on August 8, the date of departure, jeopardizing reaching Traverse City before dark. First, Nixon was to address the nation of his resignation from the presidency, a historic event that Bill insisted the family should watch on TV. That delayed leaving until after the noon hour. Second, there was a flat tire on the travel trailer close to Ludington. By the time Bill changed the tire, it was late afternoon. Assuming another three hours of travel remaining, the family decided to find an overnight site before proceeding any further. Jean studied the camping guidebook and announced that Whispering Surf Campground, located on Bass Lake, sounded like a good stop. As they turned right at the Wishing Well and drove along Lakeshore Drive, all members of the family were immediately taken with the beautiful view of Bass Lake.

The following morning Bill went to Pentwater to find a garage to fix the flat tire. Meanwhile, Elaine asked the woman at the entrance of the campground if she knew of a Kraybill household in the area. Elizabeth Kraybill was a good high school friend who lived close to the Cerny home in New York before the move to Indiana. Liz had told Elaine many stories about her Bass Lake vacations in Michigan. Surprisingly, the woman said, "Yes!" and directed Elaine to the Kraybill summer home on Lakeshore Drive. Imagine Elaine's delight in seeing Liz sitting in the front yard that morning!

The following day Liz's father, Dick Kraybill, invited the Cerny family to sail with him on his O'Day sailboat. Mr. Kraybill, an excellent sailor, gave the Cernys a tour of the lake, whetting their appetite for sailing themselves. The family was told about the Bass Lake Sailing Club that raced for two weeks and which all were invited to join.

Traveling to Traverse City quickly became a distant memory. The clincher was Bill's introduction to a new sport—salmon fishing! A campsite neighbor invited Bill to fish in his eighteen-foot boat. They launched the boat in Pentwater Lake, headed west for several miles in Lake Michigan, then trolled about in wide loops. They caught several fish. Bill was hooked!

Bass Lake, the quaint village of Pentwater, beaches, swimming, boating, the Outlet, waterskiing, sailing, salmon fishing, friends. These were the initial attractions and since then, many more have been added.

In 1982, Bill and Marian purchased property and built a cottage. Later, Mary and Jean added homes for their families. All four daughters continue to vacation at Bass Lake every year, which now includes spouses, children, and children's children.

My Story: Lookout Cottage on Thiele Road
—Christine Torp Payleitner

My great-grandfather, Ernst Theo Behr, was a German-born and trained mural artist based out of Chicago. He maintained studios downtown from 1887 until his death in 1922. Every summer the Behr family, and other artists, vacationed and worked in areas like Lake Geneva, Wisconsin. One year he and his friends went to a place called Lookout Cottage on Thiele Road in Bass Lake, Michigan. So impressed by his father's descriptions of Bass Lake, son Herbert Behr began thinking seriously about the place.

E. Theo became very ill in 1921. A private nurse, Bessie Craig, was hired to care for him until his death on March 9, 1922. Herbert and Bessie were married that May and honeymooned at the cottage. The family completed the purchase of it on August 24, 1922. Many happy years have been spent vacationing with their family and future generations. Several generations have honeymooned in the cottage.

I've always found a certain magic in the woods—no doubt. During earlier summers here, folks enjoyed fortnightly dances at Camp Morrison. For all generations, days were spent with lifelong friends and family on the beach, or threats of ghost stories and snipe hunts in the evenings. So many hours spent in various types of boats looking for turtles, sailing, and getting sunburned. Skinny dipping and wearing poison-ivy clothes afterward were also possibilities.

Time seemed to stand still at the cottage. So many interesting places to explore—The Three Sisters, Kibby Creek, the Lighthouse Channel Rocks, the cemeteries, Devil's Hole, King's Canyon, bandshell evenings, the building of Consumers Power, and my grandparents' house and attic in Pentwater. Above all, there was Auntie Rie's Playhouse.

Five little girls reenacted the Boxcar Children stories in a shoebox-sized space and somehow fit! Our stories were original, our imaginations fully engaged, and we learned more about ourselves than we realized. We celebrated black-and-white family movies and *The Adventures of the Pump House Toad* with loads of popcorn. Thursday evenings would not have been complete without families enjoying root-beer floats and building houses of cards.

How many times did everyone dig the Outlet channel out or watch satellites go by overhead while looking for shooting stars? I really miss seeing the aurora borealis at night. We still go out as a family to watch the sunset, look at stars and planets, and search the beach for treasured rocks.

Now, over one hundred years later, life on our point in the Outlet still has its own magic. Every year brings new challenges of fitting into and maintaining the "Old Girl"—as I tend to think of the cottage. We are grateful for whatever inspiration brought E. Theo Behr here.

My Story: The Love I Have for Bass Lake
—Wendy Wanzer Jonkers

The love I have for Bass Lake was passed down to me from my parents, grandparents, and great-grandparents, almost as if it were a part of my DNA, and every bit as much a part of my gene pool as the red hair and freckles that have dotted the faces of members of each generation of my family. From the first glimpse of Bass Lake by Lakeshore Drive each summer, my memories and scenes of the stories I've heard from my parents come to my mind, like snippets of old home movies, clips playing out in my imagination as I make my way around the west side of Bass Lake.

The cottage that my dad's grandfather built and that we stayed in for a few summers when I was young comes into view. For over a hundred years the cottage was green, and now it isn't, but that doesn't change the happy memories I have of being there with my extended family, many of whom still have legacy cottages nearby.

The Wrights' cottage is just down the road, and I see their Sunfish anchored near the shore. I remember when I was about five years old, and Carolyn Wright Olson had generously lent my dad their Sunfish to take my brother and me on our first sail. My father, who had sailed his whole life on Bass Lake, albeit on an old wooden Crescent, also invited his sister, and off we went. What was my dad thinking? Four people on a Sunfish? But what did I know? Our sail started off very pleasantly, but as the wind picked up and we started to heel, I began to express my concern. Don't worry, my dad assured me, I've never capsized. Five minutes later we were all in the drink. I still remember the feel of those Bass Lake weeds wrapping around my legs as I floated in the water. This little mishap didn't deter me from delighting in a lifetime of sailing a Sunfish. Teaching me to sail on Bass Lake was one of the greatest gifts my dad could have given me, and I think of him every time I'm out there.

Passing over the Outlet bridge, I think of my mother, Gwendolyn Sybeson, and her family during the 1930s staying in Mrs. Parbs's Outlet channel cottages, fondly referred to as Sunbeam and Moonbeam. Just across the road on the way to the beach one day, a young boy was hiding behind a tree, watching silently at the group passing by. The redheaded, freckle-faced boy didn't escape my great aunt's notice, and she asked, "Isn't that the Wanzer boy?" More than twenty years later, my mom's aunt ran into my dad's mom in Memphis, where they all lived, and they fondly reminisced about their shared Bass Lake history. An invitation to dinner led to a courtship and marriage, and then the opportunity for my parents to take their own children to Bass Lake and share with them the things they had loved in their younger days.

In the house just down the road lived the Brower family, and my seventeen-year-old father and Buzz Brower enlisted in the Marines together on July 19, 1945. My dad wanted to do his part in the war effort and had long admired the Marines (he had, after all, named his sailboat Devil Dog), so the pair took off for the recruiting station in Grand Rapids, were sworn in, transported to Detroit, and then off to basic training at Parris Island the next day. Leaving behind his buddies, Don Lambrix and Teddy Behr, I'm sure my dad had second thoughts about his early exit from Bass Lake in the peak of summer season, but he returned that fall after boot camp, wearing his green fatigues, and he tried to make up for lost time at the lake.

The joy of being at Bass Lake is as much about the people who surround us as it is about the beautiful lake, tranquil woods, and sugar sand beach. After a lifetime of being at Bass Lake, I'm still amazed at the new people I meet each year who also have a long Bass Lake history, and our bond is almost instantaneous because we share some of the same experiences and the same common ground.

Many descendants of those early family resorters have kept up the tradition of Bass Lake summers. My dad used to joke that we had cousins by the dozens around Bass Lake and Pentwater. For the first ten years of our marriage, every time he met someone new, my husband, Craig, would ask if we were related to them. Our children knew the joy of spending time with their grandparents at Bass Lake each summer, and now our grandchildren can do the same. Someday when they're older, they'll be able to look back at old pictures of their family members at Bass Lake and understand why we all look a little more sun-kissed, a little happier, a little more content, and very much at peace when we're at Bass Lake.

My Story: The Beauty of Sailing
—Julie Achenbaum

Some of my fondest memories of Bass Lake are with my grandfather, Charlie Barrow, sailing on the lake. It was a special time that we spent together, just the two of us, and I cherished it each summer. During those moments, he taught me a lot about boats, wind direction, and lake life, but the most important lessons I learned from him were about confidence and gratitude.

When we arrived at the racing checkpoint, we'd usually have some time before getting going when the sailors were docking their boats and scoping out the course. This was always a special time for me because I got to see my grandfather in his glory. He was up at the lake, one of his favorite places on earth, preparing for a sailboat race, surrounded by longtime local friends. He was the epitome of friendliness, and this became evident to me as I watched him converse and exchange jokes with members of the Bass Lake Sailing Club.

He loved it when the Butterfly fleet was plentiful since it was always overshadowed by the Sunfish fleet. I recall a race that he knew was going to be tricky and observed, "Look at that strong north wind—we're going to have to be careful jibing around the third buoy." He had plotted out the entire race in his head and knew with great certainty what challenges were ahead. That was the type of person he was: calm, prepared, and instilling a sense of confidence in me. Although I was nervous that day, I tried not to let on, and deep down, I knew we'd be just fine with him guiding us.

When the race horn blew, we set off on a run with the wind carrying us at top speed. "What a spectacular wind we've got today," he remarked as we set off toward the first buoy. I watched him carefully let the sail out and gaze up at the empty milk jug that was tied to the top of the mast, blowing carefully in the wind.

He exhaled deeply as if to communicate his happiness in that moment, enjoying the gorgeous weather, and taking in the sweet smell of summer that flowed through the steady breeze. We were sailing, and on a perfect day like today, he was grateful. And by extension, I was grateful because these moments of calm and beauty were not an everyday occurrence, and they were meant to be appreciated and experienced fully. My grandfather showed me this.

As we approached the third buoy, I sat nervously on the bow of the boat with my legs straddling the centerboard, ready for my tasks. I was the ideal first mate because I was so lightweight and therefore didn't create any additional drag in the water. We sailed toward the orange marker, and I watched him at the helm, calmly tightening the sail and pushing the tiller toward port, preparing to jibe. "Coming about!" he exclaimed.

"Ready!" I replied as I pulled up the centerboard to clear off the weeds and simultaneously ducked my head in preparation for the swing of the boom. The boom whooshed across the boat and the sail filled on the other side. My uncertainty and nervousness were heavy until I caught his eye underneath his navy-blue captain's hat. "Okay?" he said, with a grin on his face. "Only one more to go." Instantaneously, I felt calm, with a renewed sense of certainty because he put me at ease. Each time we went for a sail he gradually relinquished greater responsibility to me, and I grew more confident in my own abilities. I'm certain I would not be the confident sailor or person I am today without having him leading by example.

I feel so fortunate to have shared so many memories like these with my grandfather. He showed me the value of being kind to others and appreciating the world for all its wondrous gifts. I only hope that I'm able to instill the same values in my sons that he instilled in me and honor his legacy by one day teaching them the beauty of sailing.

Our Story: The Fieldstone Cottage
—Dave and Beth Walden

One of the most unique and recognizable cottages on Bass Lake is about a half mile north of the Wishing Well, at 7307 South Lakeshore Drive. Most people instantly recognize the cottage with the fieldstone fence and foundation. It has been known by many names over the years. Its original name was "Here You Are—There You Go." It has also been known as "The

Ship House," "The Monkey House," and "The Hobbit House."

It was originally built as a fishing cottage in 1920 by Dr. C.F. Crosby of Maywood, Illinois. He enjoyed relaxing and fishing on beautiful Bass Lake. He was an amateur artist and painted several wildlife scenes on the inside cabin walls, two of which still exist. Dr. Crosby died unexpectedly, and his widow sold the property to George Steindrager of Michigan City, Indiana, in 1928.

George Steindrager owned a Michigan City gas station and spent a lot of his free time up at the lake fishing and envisioning the future of the cottage. It is said it took ten hours to get from Michigan City to Bass Lake in the 1930s via mostly two-track dirt roads. The cottage was significantly expanded in the 1950s. George was an amateur mason, who, along with his children and grandchildren, collected the fieldstones over many summers.

He built the breakfast nook, south addition, and added the stone foundations and stone fences, giving the cabin its current footprint.

After his death, the cottage went to his children. His daughter, Dorothy, even lived in it year-round for a while. After that, Georgia (George's granddaughter) and Harry Wolter of Michigan City took ownership. They, along with their children, did a significant number of repairs and upgrading of the cottage. Eventually, the cottage was sold to Beth and Dave Walden of Shakopee, Minnesota, in 2015.

The Waldens continue to make repairs and updates to the cottage each summer. In 2020, they moved from Minnesota to Valparaiso, Indiana. This reduced their "commute" time from twelve hours to three hours, much more manageable. In the fall of 2020, the Wolter family joined them to celebrate the centennial year of the cottage. It was special to have them with us. We hope to be blessed to spend many more summers at the cottage!

My Story: Our Walk Through the Woods
—Charlotte Gilbert Drayer

This Christmas I received two gifts that included an image that I took at the lake last year that I had shared with my family and a few friends. I wrote "the lake" because that's how we've always referred to our summer cottages, built by my widowed great-grandmother, Bertha Louise Parsons Finch. She built the first cottage in 1904, then three more in the 1920s, as a less expensive place to stay in the summers when she wasn't teaching fourth grade in Chicago. They were also a summer income source for her.

When Granny was given the one-hundred-by-five-hundred-foot lakefront lot by Pray, the developer, to "salt" the southwest side of Bass Lake with cottages to spur development there, the glacial sand dunes had trees the height of my grandfather, who was six years old at the time. The land had been clear-cut of the old-growth oak and white pine trees to rebuild Chicago after the Great Fire on October 8–10, 1871. The loggers took everything with a market value, leaving only commercially worthless wood, like beech trees, behind. Among those rare old trees were lots of little jack pines. Their resinous cones open to spread their seeds when exposed to fire or intense sun, which they got when the forest was gone. Those trees are not commercially useful and never get large. These trees, little sassafras trees, small oaks, and white pines were most prevalent in the woods when I was growing up in the fifties and sixties. Today you wouldn't know that the forest is second-growth because the white pines and the red, white, and black oaks are so large.

> "It was important to me that they love Bass Lake as much as I did. It is where I'm grounded."
> —Charlotte Drayer

There are several ways to get to Lake Michigan from the cottages. You can drive, bike, or walk north along the lake, then cut west down a lane, and finally walk down the dunes from the parking area. You can kayak, paddle a canoe, row, or motor north along the lake to the Outlet, then continue through the Outlet to the weir before walking along the stream that courses through the sand to the big lake. Finally, if you're fit, you can walk through the woods over substantial dunes to Sunset Beach. From there, you can walk on the shore to the Outlet beach or stay and play at Sunset. The Outlet beach is broader, and the warmer, shallow stream attracts children.

I was also glad to hike through the woods to the beach, where we went every afternoon around 2:00 p.m. unless it was raining. I knew the way by heart by the time I was eight or nine. The path wasn't always obvious. At the east end the route started at the Bird House's west door by going straight up the dune called Fairview, then you took the left fork in the path on the west side of the hill. Part of the route was over an old, sand tote road built for access to the oil wells that were there when Mom was young. In the deepest part of the woods, however, it was so dark that there was little understory and there was so much leaf litter on the ground that there was no path. The route ended at Sunset Beach, south of the Outlet beach. We learned that route so well that my cousin Allyson and I as preteens were allowed to carry our lunches through the woods to the beach to eat there, then meet our families at the Outlet later. We weren't allowed to swim until the rest of the family arrived because Lake Michigan has strong longshore currents, undertows that can pull your legs out from under you and carry you north very quickly.

The wooded sand dunes between Bass Lake and Lake Michigan are substantial. We call them Eagle Top, Middle Hill, and Baldy, but mariners call them The Three Sisters because they are easily recognizable far out on the lake and are used for navigation. The hike through the woods to Lake Michigan involves climbing the shoulder between two of those dunes. It's steep and slippery because of all of the leaves on the slope. Oak leaves decompose slowly and slide across each other. As kids, the steepest and longest slope had three trees down across that part of the route, about halfway up the slope. We referred to that as "Gramps's Resting Spot." We all availed ourselves of a rest at that place, sitting on the logs. Then we'd push on. At the top there was a big old beech tree with generations of initials carved into it, including those of my parents and grandparents. It was mostly downhill to the beach from there.

As Gramps, George Britton Finch, who was in the advertising film business with the Jam Handy Organization, would say, it was a "soft fadeout."

My Story: Operation Whitewash
—Molly Allen-Doster

The old, white dock had been in the family for years. One summer my Aunt Ginny and Uncle Dan decided to paint it green. This made all the kids mad because the dock had always been white, and after complaining all summer, we finally decided to act. Our parents were going to pick up my grandma at the airport one evening—they told us they'd be back at

11:00 p.m. It was the perfect night to carry out our devious plan. After they drove off, we set the can of white paint down on the dock and took a deep breath. Daredevil Emily dipped her brush and made one thick, white stroke on the green dock. She calmly remarked, "Well, it looks like we're going to have to do this after all."

There was very little room on the narrow dock, and we kept getting paint on ourselves. Finally, we used our brains and painted the dock while standing in the water. Paint flying everywhere, the extreme excitement, and little fish nibbling at my ankles—I will never forget. Our dripping wet masterpiece was finally finished at 10:15 p.m. We cleaned off our whitewashing weapons in the musty garage. The white paint on our skin we took off with turpentine.

We used soap and water on our arms and legs to try and get the paint smell off. After we dried off, we saw the bright headlights pull into the driveway. "Oh my gosh, they're back!" I yelled. We sprung up the stairs and just after we threw ourselves into a pretend card game, my mom walked in the room. "Hi, guys. What have you been up to?" she asks.

"Oh … not TOO much," I said sweetly, thinking to myself, "except to restore the sacred white dock."

My Story: Bass Lake Brigadoon
—Carla Barrow

Bass Lake reminds me of the play *Brigadoon*—a village that appears for only one day every one hundred years. The townspeople awake to simply enjoy the day. No one ages and everything stays the same, and the world is magical for those brief twenty-four hours before everyone goes back to sleep.

My fondest memory is the sound of our cottage's vintage screen door swinging back and forth. For a brief moment, I am transported back in time as a young girl dashing out the door on a mission to Lake Michigan. I remember wearing my swimsuit to bed because I couldn't wait to wake up and head for the beach—a quarter mile walk away. And endless hours swimming at the Outlet because the water was so warm.

I remember: Bill's Dune Rides in Hart, where the Scenic Ride was $1.25, and the Thrill Ride was $1.50; purchasing Coca-Cola from glass bottles for ten cents at Birdland Hardware; searching for shooting stars darting about the night sky; and sleeping like a baby because everything was so dark, still, and quiet. Rainy days inevitably prompted marathon Monopoly game challenges, along with ping-pong set up in the garage. I also remember getting lost in a book, sometimes for days.

When we first arrived, my mother immediately went into town to retrieve the upcoming movie schedule. This was decades before VHS and DVDs, and she loved catching up on all the movies she had missed that year. But one year we arrived, and the theater had closed. It was inevitable but heartbreaking and we were devastated. The good news is that the giant red stand-alone popcorn machine found a new home at the grocery store in Hart, and the legacy lives on.

There was no social media and the only communication we had for a month with friends back home was through letters. We did not have a phone or television. I remember my father driving to the Wishing Well phone booth to call work. Finally, his employer insisted that we install a phone, but that wasn't until the early 1970s.

These collective experiences might be profound and others simply pleasurable. You recall traditions, rituals, and celebrations along with chores and the occasional boredom. Each year you came back a little older. Most importantly you made mistakes and learned and grew as a result—but the lake never changed.

My Story: First View from the Dock
—Barbara Barrow Achenbaum

It's the dock—when I drive up to Bass Lake for the first visit of the summer, I still spring out of the car and hasten to the end of the dock. With a deep sigh, I take it all in—the birds chirping, the water lapping on the shore, the sun glistening on the lake, the cloudless cerulean sky—and memories flood back. I'm in my seventh decade now—but I feel like I'm five again.

I recall that first motorboat ride of the season down the Outlet like it was yesterday—spotting dangling tree branches that had succumbed to winter storms, scouting for sunning turtles, and finally catching that first glimpse of the Big Lake. Always the same questions in my mind: how wide is the sandy beach this year? How much have the dunes shifted? Is the

Outlet flowing? And even: is there a second sandbar to swim out to?

Satisfied with the new summer's version of the landscape, I make the return trip home, stopping to surreptitiously snatch a few yellow blossoms from the green carpet of lily pads (despite the persistent rumor that it is illegal). As we leave the no-wake zone, I open up the throttle, steer the boat around the bend, and then it clearly comes into view—our dock with its American flag proudly waving.

Back on land, I venture up the overgrown pathway of ferns toward the rambling white clapboard cottage, which has been in the family for seventy-five years. As children, my two older sisters and I were fortunate enough to spend the month of August here—and, like the generations before us, to create vivid and lasting memories.

From the cottage porch, in my mind, I make out the vista of my parents—decades earlier—enjoying their evening cocktail, relaxing after a day of boating and beaching and preparing our favorite dinner—grilled fresh fish from Bortell's, ripe tomatoes rich in flavor, and corn that was picked just that morning.

I think back to many starry, moonless nights where the sky was an explosion of constellations—and I was struck by the unexpected thrill of a falling star. I remember one exciting evening when I was five—lying on a cozy blanket, my parents paddling our canoe to the middle of the lake, where we took in the brilliant kaleidoscope of the northern lights.

And now I'm seven and my sisters and I are having sandwiches on the dock. Suddenly, we see the Day Sailer, trailed by a beautiful line of sailboats racing across the lake, rounding the second buoy. Dad was almost always dead last in the Butterfly fleet. Still, we relished the annual awards ceremony at Summit Park Pavilion, where we proudly collected his few hand-sewn cloth butterflies.

Fast forward to age ten. My sisters and I are "fishing" off the dock, throwing breadcrumbs into the water, attracting a swarming crowd of tiny bluegills, capturing them in large nets, and then deftly pulling them out. My oldest sister bravely grasps the squirming creatures and quickly returns them to the lake, where they become easy prey once again.

And now I see myself at twelve—at the helm of our 6-hp motorboat bombing around the lake at full speed, enjoying the thrill, the independence, and the wind whipping through my hair. In truth, getting my driver's license a few years later paled in comparison.

From the water, I spy my bikini-clad sisters on the dock—slathering on baby oil to cultivate that perfect tan, listening to WOKY on the radio, and devouring beauty tips from *Seventeen* magazine, picked up at Fort Dahl on our weekly trip to "Big Lud."

And now my sisters are floating on a bright pink blow-up raft, waiting for the moment when they are just hot enough to take a refreshing dip in the lake. I loved when they embarked on one of their daring rituals—skinny dipping or washing their hair—the soapy bubbles drifting away and disappearing in the weeds.

Suddenly, it's me on that dock, a young mother stealing some quiet time and a cup of coffee before my three young daughters wake and begin asking which of the treasured adventures we will do today—climb Eagle Top, race cars at AJ's, play mini-golf at Rinaldi's, or gobble down ice cream at the House of Flavors.

Looking from the ice cream shop across Hancock Street to the bandshell, in my mind, the Thursday evening band concert comes to life—kids frolicking, parents enjoying glasses of wine and sharing this year's gossip, teens gathering by the yacht club to smoke forbidden cigarettes, and then the band playing "Good Night, Ladies," a sign that another magical evening is coming to a close.

On a different morning a decade later, again armed with coffee, I tiptoe down to the dock and watch the sun gently rise over the trees—its bright yellow glory preceded by wispy clouds of pink, gold, and violet. I sit down and open my book and am startled by the whisper of an approaching flatboat, whose mini chairs hold dedicated fishermen, uttering the briefest of good mornings as they quietly drift past.

And next comes the appearance of the swans, gliding over from their home on the lush, uninhabited nearby shore. I recall the first sighting each summer—looking to see how many babies there were—and then, as the weeks go by, watching their feathers gradually turn from gray to white.

Today I'm in my seventh decade, and my first visit to the dock still fills me with great joy. I look eastward at the vista, and it remains sweeping and colorful and gorgeous and unchanged. Of course, I can't ignore the features that were not there during my childhood—the occasional din of a truck on "new" 31, the many houses that have sprung up across the lake, and now the looming, white wind turbines doing their elegant twirling dance.

I think about the generations in our family, imagining each of them taking their annual first look at the lake. My grandfather, who purchased Franklin's Folly in 1940 on a lark; my father, who earned college money selling bass caught in Lake Michigan to local farmers; my daughters, who despite living one thousand miles away, insist that a summer is not complete without that cocktail hour on the dock; and now my young grandchildren, who are content to build sandcastles on our tiny beach and to tiptoe into the water. I imagine them cultivating their own special memories in the years ahead.

For all of us, in its own way, that unique, personal, and priceless quality of the first view will endure. I learned this best when I made a trip a few years ago with my father, who was near the end of his life. He was suffering from many challenges, including much weakened vision. I pushed his wheelchair out to the end of the dock. And there it appeared on his glowing face—despite the nine decades flown by and the infirmities—that moment of recognition. The sounds, the smells, the dimmest glimpse of blue water—and he was five years old again.

My Story: My Grandma's Wisdom
—Charlie Danoff

Bass Lake memories appear whenever the family gathers around the original maple dining table. Discussions covered a wide range of topics, from what to order from Bortell's the next day for lunch to stories from my grandparents about days gone by. Tales were told about my grandpa's enterprising fishing business with childhood pals Harry Hillman and Marty McKevitt during the 1940s. After dinner we would retire to the living room for group games of Michigan rummy on the green tablecloth or perhaps Chinese checkers. My memory is fuzzy on who won which games. We listened to classical music from nearby Interlochen Public Radio all day long.

I remember my grandma engaging authentically and never talking down to us as kids. She was genuinely interested in her grandchildren's point of view. Today I appreciate the candor of our conversations. If a disagreement ensued, she showed us how to defend our point of view.

She was also a lifelong learner and regularly brought *The Great Courses on Tape* for the drive from Chicago to Pentwater. She was teaching us by example that education does not stop after you get a diploma. She advised us that "material things break" and imparted her wisdom that there were bigger fish to fry—in the worrying business. I bet we ate some delicious freshly deep-fried smelt from Bortell's for lunch that day.

Watching the sunset at the Outlet—the conclusion of another delightful Bass Lake summer day.

Chapter 12

Bass Lake Farewell

A lot of things have changed but this has not—the urge to come back every year. I could live at Bass Lake and never get tired of it. When we must leave, I always ask myself the same question: Do you think Bass Lake will be the same next year? Every year when I come back, a tree might have been cut down or a cottage built, but the beauty and friendliness remain the same.

—Bob Thompson

The saddest day of the summer is when the toys are all put away, the boats are out of the water, and it's time to say goodbye to the cottage and Bass Lake until the next summer. The Haigh family had a tradition that no one could speak or plan of Bass Lake until after Christmas each year. Some adults have been known to get absolutely giddy with excitement on the eve of their return to Bass Lake each summer.

Last Time
—Anne Kraybill Krecko

It is hard to leave Bass Lake. In the Kraybill family there was an unwritten "last time" list. Last time to browse Gustafson's. Last time to eat an ice cream cone at the House of Flavors. Last time to buy glass animals at Birdland. Last time to hike on Bill's Trail ... go to the beach ... buy candy at the Wishing Well.

On the very last day we would pluck a sassafras leaf, sniff it, and put it between the pages of a book to take home. We would nibble on a tiny, fragrant wintergreen leaf. And, of course, we would say a final goodbye to the lake.

One August when I was in my teens I sneaked down to the water while

111

my parents finished packing up the car and hitching up our sailboat, Ondine, for the drive back to Rochester, New York. I started goofing off in the lake and somehow my glasses flew off my face. They just disappeared. My parents gave me a few minutes to look for them, but it was a late start and they finally said, "Anne, it's time to get in the car and go!"

About twenty-five years later I got a call from my dad, who said he felt something under his foot in Bass Lake. It was a pair of glasses, and he wondered if they might be mine. I have an eye condition, strabismus, which makes it hard to focus both eyes on one image. Though the glasses had faded from tortoise brown to a dull grayish blue, the years in Bass Lake had not changed the thick lenses full of prisms.

On a wall of the Crows Nest, our Bass Lake cottage, there hangs a small shadowbox displaying my glasses. It is a reminder to me that while life changes, Bass Lake stays pretty much the same.

The Swing: Bass Lake Farewell

Alice M. Kimball was a high-school classmate and fellow teacher of Bertha Finch in the Chicago-area schools in the early 1900s. Soon after Bertha built her second Bass Lake cottage, Alice purchased land just to the south and, in her retirement, built a cottage she named Wabun. Every summer, Alice enjoyed entertaining family and friends and sharing the beauty of Bass Lake with them. Years later, Alice sold the cottage to George and Alice Finch.

Nearly fifty years later, George and Alice's son, John, and his wife, Dorothy, were at a local bank in Ludington cashing a check. When the teller saw their names, she asked if they were the Finches of Finchaven at Bass Lake. When they replied that indeed they were, she excused herself briefly and returned with a notebook containing the writings of Alice Kimball about Bass Lake from the perspective of her cottage, Wabun. How the teller came to be in possession of Miss Kimball's writings remains a mystery, but the notebook came home with the Finches that day, and it remains in the cottage that inspired the stories that give us a glimpse into how a Bass Lake cottage might view the family that breathes life into that dwelling and makes it a home.

September 10 - 1952

To return to a well-loved spot after the lapse of years is often a saddening experience. But this visit to Finehaven has not been so. To be sure, there are changes in the neighborhood that have not been happy ones. How I regret the passing of the Indian Landing that we knew!

But at Finehaven-Wabun to me — the changes have all been by way of added convenience - the old values are intact - the same dear old neighbors and friends, the blue lake, the sunset flush in the eastern sky, the cathedral of the woods, the essences of peace, simplicity, remoteness from the world's tumult. All are here, and it has been a happy time for me. -

Alice M. Kimball

Alice Kimball reflects on the end of an era. Some things may change, yet Bass Lake remains the same.

Following is the final entry into Miss Kimball's notebook, and it poignantly portrays the quietness after the chaos and those end-of-summer feelings of Bass Lakers who must say farewell until next summer.

It was very still at Wabun. The warm afternoon sunshine, filtering through the leaves, lay in a lovely pattern of light and shade about her as she sat there in the seat Jim had built out under the trees. The rasping note of the cicada was in the air, and the faint put-put of a motorboat came to her from across the lake; but these did not break the stillness, they only seemed to make the silence audible.

It had been a full, happy summer. Now for the first time she had a chance to sit here by herself and think it over. A chance to look out through the trees to the end of the pier and John Finch's boat anchored a little way out; to glance up the road toward the March cottage and the Shelton Wright's, good friends of many a summer; and to think how much all this meant to her. A chance to recall the comings and goings of the people she loved.

A book lay on the seat beside her. It was quite a big book, and its pages held names and dates beginning a-way back in Wabun's first year. It held more than these—there were drawings, jingles and quips reminiscent of special frolics; there were pressed flowers of the North country with penciled notes to tell when and where they were found; and there were snapshots, dozens of them, that made her laugh or perhaps cry.

She had been looking through, but now she laid it down, to consider certain small signs she had noticed in the last few days—the "shape of things to come."

Yesterday, walking back from the Lewis farm, she had seen asters and goldenrod in full bloom by the roadside, and milkweed with the pods already formed.

This morning, down at the Outlet, it suddenly struck her that there were no red-winged blackbirds about. A few days ago, there had been hundreds of them!

Looking over toward the swing, her eyes rested on one leaf standing out on the sassafras tree, marked with tell-tale splotches of blood-red.

A car passed on the road below, on its way out of the woods. It was full of people and luggage; fishing poles protruded from the back, and it carried a canoe on top. She did not know the people, but she knew their destination as surely as though they had carried a placard screaming "Back to Town!"

She took up the book and began to write:

August 25, 1941

The family went home yesterday. In a tumult of good-byes and waving hands, the car slid out of sight among the trees, overflowing with girls, grown-ups, dogs, luggage, wraps, lady's-slipper roots for transplanting, jars of blueberries and sundry other spoils of the North Woods. For the first time in weeks, no bathing suits drape the clothesline. The swing hangs empty and listless throughout the quiet afternoon.

What a turbulent life that swing has had! Up in the air and down; one, two, sometimes three pairs of legs pumping madly, or waving wildly untoward the trees, or feet dragging, "letting the old cat die." More than once, it had been the center of a rousing combat, or the goal of a mad race for possession. And often during this last summer, two little girls had occupied it together—Virginia with a protecting arm around little Mary Joy—such a lovely name!—the winning little child who had called out all the latent mothering instinct in Virginia and given it a happy outlet. That tender picture would remain, one of the lasting associations hovering around the old swing. But now that too has passed. Now it has in prospect long, still days of quietness, in which it may rest and look forward to next summer and the children's return.

What of next summer? Twelve and Sixteen have found the old swing not too childish for their pleasure; it has been a good comrade in their sport. Will Thirteen and Seventeen love it as well? Or will it be pushed back gently into the Heaven of Outgrown Toys, along with the mosquito nets from long ago campings on Fairview, wreckage of the raft Steve and Edwin built, Bobbie's horseshoes, John's toy boats, Sybil's paper dolls, Billy's butterfly net, Virginia's paddle?

Must an old swing be content to hang empty and motionless in that land of Forever Past—just remembering?

The pages of this book recall more than a century of treasured life at Bass Lake. And the story continues. Today, thanks to technology, memories can be shared in an instant with those far away. As Bass Lakers add to their personal histories, the lake, the woods, and the Outlet beach are merely enchanting backdrops where happy moments are captured and remembered. The story continues each year as family and friends, old and new, gather around the picnic table, a campfire, or on a leisurely boat tour. Bass Lake is like an old friend saying, "Welcome back."

So long for now. See you at the lake.

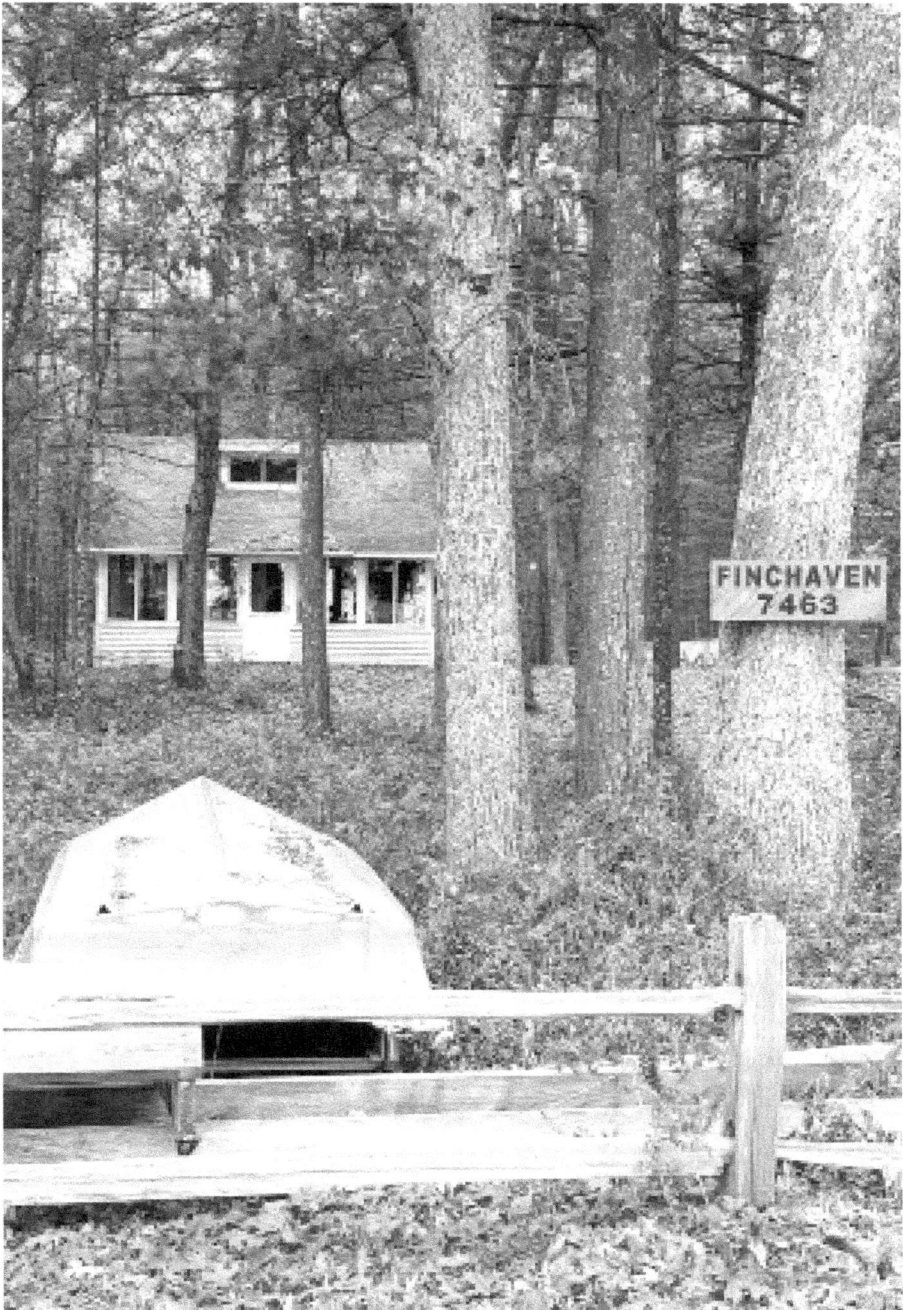

Closed for the season. Finchaven, formerly Wabun, hibernates until next spring.

By the Way ...

In 1926, the Bortell family donated Bortell's Landing—just across from today's Bortell's Fisheries restaurant—to create what is now Summit Park on the shore of Lake Michigan.

The Purple Gang, a ruthless group of mobsters from Detroit who operated from 1921 to 1932 (during the 1920s Prohibition era), came to the Bass Lake area for rest and refreshment, often staying at Camp Morrison.

Marie Hillman offered school on the front porch of her cottage in September of 1937 for Bass Lake-area children who didn't return to Chicago during the height of the polio outbreak.

Many logging and oil trails crisscrossed the Wright property behind Finchaven. Hank Gilbert recalled the intrusion of the oil well known as Big Jean. In the 1940s, his parents were sitting on a little hill to the left as you entered the clearing, and they watched the Big Jean oil well come in. The owners of the nearby cottage, Broadview, had just painted their fence, which they had repurposed from the World's Fair, with a white zinc-based paint. The gas that was released when the oil well came in immediately turned the white fence black. The Broadview owners were upset, and the oil well people paid for the fence to be repainted.

Playboy magazine did a photoshoot at the Bass Lake Outlet on Lake Michigan during the summer of 1963, and both the models and crew stayed at Dick Guenther's cottage. The layout appeared in a fall edition of the magazine, which made the rounds at a Bass Lake cocktail party the following summer. Those in attendance commented positively on how well written the article was and how good the Outlet looked in the photos.

In 1976, Smert's Resort had a close call when a tornado briefly touched down, uprooting large trees and smashing the roof of a car. The short-lived twister came across Bass Lake, then disappeared after damaging more trees and leaving the area without electricity and phone service.

A five-hour siege ended peacefully and without injury at a rental cottage on Lattin Road on March 23, 1978, after multiple shots were fired. Upon his surrender, the suspect told a reporter that he had fired the shots to get attention, but the pending narcotics charge may better explain the "why" of the situation. Bob and Ashley Gannett had just months earlier purchased the property, which included the rental cottage. As the Gannetts had earlier planned which improvements they wanted to make to their future retirement home, removing bullets from the walls and ceilings had most certainly not been on that list.

In October 2012, the Wishing Well convenience store and gas station was robbed by two men who crashed a stolen truck into the front of the convenience store. They stole liquor and cigarettes and were quickly apprehended. The resulting damage closed the store for more than two years. Under new ownership, the building was refurbished and reopened April 1, 2015, as the Wishing Well EZ Mart and gas station. Established in 1946, the Wishing Well was one of the few Bass Lake premises with public phones, a modern convenience used by many Bass Lake residents. The iconic Wishing Well, dug in 1948 south of the store, still exists … but don't drink the water!

HGTV's *House Hunters* aired an episode, "Michigan Couple with Three Kids Seeks Lakefront Vacation Cottage" on June 19, 2016, featuring a cottage on the southwestern shore of Bass Lake. The cottage was originally built in 1904 by Edwin T. Wanzer, sold to Sidney A. March in the 1930s, and subsequently was owned by three generations of the March and Cutler families before being sold in 2015.

Bass Lake Legends

Devil's Pond

Devil's Pond (sometimes referred to as Devil's Swamp) is an I-wouldn't-go-in-there, boggy, mosquito-ridden, unique ecological wonder found on the northwest side of Bass Lake. It contains floating sphagnum, a peat bog, tamarack, cranberry, and pitcher plants. Pond water flows into Kibby Creek, then Bass Lake. From Lattin Road, all you see is heavy vegetation and a lot of dead trees. Devil's Pond is as dark as black coffee and looks like it couldn't support life of any kind. Yet adventurous fishermen have gone in, catching black-colored fish.

Growing up, Kyle Chapman's family was told stories about Devil's Pond by their uncle, Bob Plummer. The most common one was that he and a friend carried a boat back to the pond to explore the area, as he had heard it was bottomless. Once on the water, they dropped an anchor with a two-hundred-foot rope, and the line pulled tight, indicating it was at least that deep. Kyle and his brother decided to confirm Uncle Bob's claim. After applying lots of mosquito repellent, they hiked to Devil's Pond. As they came into sight of open water, they realized that the ground was spongy and moving with every step. As they got closer to the water's edge, they could see that they had been walking on floating vegetation. The brothers realized that if they fell through, they might get stuck on the roots. They carefully retreated from Devil's Pond, never to return. From then on, they believed all Devil's Pond stories.

Swampy Mike

Swampy Mike is a scary character who roams the woods and can even swim! He's known to the McKevitt, Haigh, Hansford, Johnson, and Rischar families … and perhaps others. It's said he lives in Devil's Pond. Swampy Mike could show up anywhere, anytime. All you have to do is walk in a certain wooded area, ring a bell three times, and Swampy Mike will soon appear. It's also believed Swampy Mike eats garbage from the Summit Township transfer site. And children had better be good or Swampy Mike might eat you, too! It's said the Rischar family knows a bit more about the origins of Swampy Mike. And of course, these stories are best told at night.

Screen-Cutters

Screen-Cutters occasionally show up at the Chapman cottage and Karaway Kabin. Oftentimes younger family members slept on screened-in porches with roll-down canvas blinds on the inside. The children were told that if they didn't behave, the Screen-Cutters would get you! The Screen-Cutters threat proved an effective deterrent to bad behavior. But as families grew, older siblings used the threat to tease younger ones. To this day, only the brave sleep on the screened-in porches.

Appendix

Bass Lake Timeline

1850s: Beginnings of the Village of Pentwater
1855: Lumber baron Charles Mears built a sawmill in Middlesex (later it became Pentwater).
1858: Ferry service using a wooden scow-and-cable system began in Pentwater, allowing passengers to cross the channel flowing from Pentwater Lake into Lake Michigan.

1860–1870s: Pentwater incorporates and logging industry takes off
1867: In March 1867, the Village of Pentwater was incorporated.
1868: The federal government began a twenty-year project to widen and deepen the Pentwater channel, enabling more commerce.
1871: The year of the Great Chicago Fire, the West Michigan logging industry grew to rebuild Chicago.

1880–1890s: Bass Lake area discovered
1886: The Bass Lake Recreation Park Association was formed. Shares were sold at twenty-five dollars each, with funds used to clear a swimming beach and build resort conveniences.
1889: Fire burned nearly all Pentwater business buildings made of wood.
1891: Bass Lake Park was recorded. The plat includes approximately seventy-seven acres to provide a private recreational area for those who bought stock in the Bass Lake Recreation Park.
1891: Bass Lake Park First Addition was recorded.
1896: Gilbert's Addition to Bass Lake Park was recorded.

1900s: More Bass Lake subdivisions platted

1905: Bass Lake's Nagasaki Park was recorded.

1905: F.E. Pray & Son's Subdivision of Bass Lake Recreation Park was recorded.

1905: R.H. Little's Addition to Bass Lake Park was recorded.

1910s: Bass Lake Park Improvement Association, flu, war

1910: By this time, there were two hotels on Bass Lake—George McKee's seventeen-room Hotel McKee on the eastern shore, and Wayt's Hotel, owned by Lyman H. Wayt, on the western shore. In 1915, these hotel owners were also named caretakers to oversee properties in the off-season.

1912: Pentwater Beach Addition #5 was recorded.

1913: Camp Morrison opened on the shoreline of Bass Lake.

1914: Thiele's Addition to Bass Lake Park was recorded.

1915: Bass Lake Park Improvement Association (BLPIA) was organized. The group decided on dues of three dollars (today, ninety-one dollars). There was a log dam at the Bass Lake Outlet, but the association knew it needed improvement to protect Bass Lake and property. Thus, as it is today, one of the BLPIA's key responsibilities was to look after the dam.

1917: No BLPIA annual meeting was held, due to the meeting being called so late and lack of a quorum. Perhaps this was because the US had entered World War I in April 1917.

1918: The Great Influenza epidemic motivated many to search for a healthier life. Thus, Chicago residents Erva and Tom Schlick purchased the Hotel McKee property. With the help of their son, Claude, the family operated the hotel and cottages until 1972.

1918: BLPIA directors appointed a Camp Supplies Committee to look after milk, groceries, and the like for the resort.

1919: A request was made to the Washington, DC, postmaster for free rural mail delivery at Bass Lake.

1920s: Growing pains, and weeds

1920: A road was built to provide access to the west side of Bass Lake, benefiting visitors to Camp Morrison and cottagers.

1924: BLPIA held its annual meeting at Camp Morrison on August 7. Many things were discussed: The Pentwater postmaster agreed to provide mail service from June 1 to October 1. Speed limit signs of 10 mph could be posted through camp. Roads still needed improvement. Dues increased to ten dollars, and more members were needed. The question of having a dam was discussed. It was suggested that a satisfactory dam be built at a cost not to exceed $1,500.

1925: Work on the Bass Lake dam proceeded. It was necessary for the association to borrow the major part of the money to complete the dam. In July, BLPIA minutes show: dam material, $2,288; extras, $46.25; bridge, $13.20; labor, $4; engineer's changes, $236.05 ... total expenditure, nearly $2,600.

1925: Dr. Gilbert sent word to the BLPIA to ask that the road that ran in front of his house be placed in the back. Today, this likely explains why drivers must slow for a significant S curve shortly after turning north at the Wishing Well onto Lakeshore Drive.

1925: The Izaak Walton League suggested planting rice in Bass Lake, but this was objected to because "there were enough weeds in the lake without planting more."

1925: The Fincher's Retreat subdivision was recorded. Most Bass Lake properties are in Mason County; however, this subdivision runs along the south end of Bass Lake, in Oceana County.

1926: During the January 4 BLPIA board meeting at the Chicago-area home of Mr. and Mrs. Fred Blase, it was reported that the state of Michigan had nothing in the way of a machine to remove lake weeds. The association decided to see if the dam would have an effect on the weeds.

1927: The concrete dam at the Bass Lake Outlet collapsed. A new, more resilient dam was constructed. The BLPIA voted to buy a weed-cutter.

1928: In the spring, the BLPIA's $670 weeder to cut Bass Lake weeds was delivered. Pluto, as it was affectionately called, served to manage aquatic weeds until 1971.

1930s: Sickness

1937: A polio outbreak swept through the Chicago area, closing schools. Some Bass Lake summer residents decided to extend their lake stays.

Marie Hillman conducted school on the front porch of her Bass Lake Boulevard cottage.

1940s: Deadly storm

1940: The November 11 Armistice Day storm had a deadly impact near Pentwater. Two large lake freighters—the *Anna C. Minch* and *William B. Davock*—sank in Lake Michigan with all sailors on board. A third freighter—the *Novadoc*—was grounded at Juniper Beach, and seventeen crew members were saved by local fishermen. The Outlet channel between Lake Michigan and Bass Lake was blocked, causing flooding and damage to many cottages.

1947: Nile's Bass Lake Resort was recorded.

1947: The Pentwater Civic Band was formed. Its early performances were the inspiration for the Thursday night band concerts.

1950s: More resorts

1953: Nile's First Addition to Nile's Bass Lake Resort was recorded.

1958: Camp Morrison frontage on Bass Lake and nine housekeeping cabins were sold for Call's Resort (now Ferwerda's Bass Lake Resort).

1960s: BLPIA becomes BLPOA; Sailing Club launches

1962: Bass Lake Sailing Club races launch. Ever since, races continue every summer.

1964: Birch Harbor Subdivision was recorded.

1964: The Bass Lake Park Improvement Association (BLPIA) name changed to the Bass Lake Property Owners Association (BLPOA). Voted on at the August 22 regular annual meeting, the name change was done to conform to requirements of the State Rules of the Michigan Corporation and Securities Commission. The first BLPOA officers were H.H. Carstens, president; Hollis Tate, vice president; Mrs. K.C. Barrons, treasurer; and Marie Hillman, secretary.

1965: Birch Harbor Subdivision No. 2 was recorded.

1965: Significant repairs were made to the Bass Lake Outlet dam. Steel piling and concrete were added to repair damage on the upstream side of the dam.

1966: Bass Lake Shores Subdivision was recorded.

1967: Birchwood Hills was recorded.

1967: Reginald Yaple purchased Camp Morrison and constructed an RV campground called Whispering Surf Travel Trailer Village.

1967: A massive alewife die-off left beaches all around Lake Michigan covered with the stench of billions of dead and rotting fish. Bass Lake Outlet was not immune. The introduction of salmon and trout into Lake Michigan helped keep the future alewife population in check, leaving that summer's die-off as the worst on record.

1969: Bass Lake Shores Subdivision No. 2 was recorded.

1969: The Bass Lake dam suffered storm damage. BLPOA created its dam fund.

1969: Construction began on the Ludington Pumped Storage Plant, built north of Bass Lake. Owned by Consumers Energy and DTE Energy, the hydroelectric plant was completed in 1973.

1970s: Smert's Resort and more Bass Lake subdivisions

1972: Schlick's Bass Lake hotel property was purchased by Lea and Vince Smiertelny, who renamed it Smert's Resort on Bass Lake. By 2017, Smert's Resort was sold, and its buildings removed.

1972: Bass Lake Shores Subdivision No. 3 was recorded.

1972: The BLPOA newsletter referenced Marie Hillman's death. She had been asked to write a history of Bass Lake "since the beginning of our organization in 1886." Mrs. Mary Lambrix was to be her co-author. She went on to create a scrapbook which formed the basis of this Bass Lake history.

1973: Midland Heights Estates was recorded.

1974: North Avenue Subdivision was recorded.

1974: The Michigan Department of State Highways listened to BLPOA concerns about the new US Highway 31 running too close to Bass Lake. The route was moved further east to mitigate possible environmental impacts to the lake and creeks feeding it.

1980s: Too much water and too many weeds

1982: Beach grass was planted at the Bass Lake Outlet to help preserve the large sand dunes along the Lake Michigan shore.

1986: September 9–12 rains brought The Great Michigan Flood, a one-hundred-year rain. The Bass Lake Outlet dam embankments were severely eroded, requiring repairs. In Oceana County, the Hart Dam collapsed, causing extensive flooding. Efforts to rebuild Hart Dam started soon after.

1988: On April 27, the circuit court of Mason County vacated the injunction against the use of chemicals to treat weeds. The BLPOA moved from cutting and harvesting Bass Lake weeds to chemical treatment.

1990s: Walsh Memorial, mussels, moths, and oil well drilling

1993: Zebra mussels and gypsy moths arrive at Bass Lake.

1996: The Bea and Billy Walsh Memorial and stone were moved to Historic White Pine Village, south of Ludington. The well-liked couple summered at Bass Lake. They were lost at sea in 1946 while traveling to entertain World War II troops.

1996: Bass Lake property owners were approached regarding oil and gas drilling leases. There were no takers that we were aware of.

1998: Bass Lake Venetian Nights began. On a designated evening, residents decorated boats with lights and paraded around the lake.

2000s: Bass Lake Improvement Board established

2000: New hotel proposed for the Bass Lake area just off US Highway 31. Today, the site is a Days Inn by Wyndham.

2001: RV park proposed south of Bass Lake (current-day Hill and Hollow Campgrounds). The plans included 180 RV sites, twenty tent sites, and sixteen rustic one-room cabins.

2005: The size of the boat ramp at Bass Lake Boulevard and Lattin Road was legally defined.

2006: Bass Lake Improvement Board (BLIB) is approved by Summit Township to manage weed treatments. The BLIB is a separate entity from BLPOA.

2009: Construction of a wind turbine farm in Lake Michigan was proposed by Scandia Corp. of Denmark. The Pentwater community created a "No Mistake in the Lake" campaign, which ended the ill-fated project.

2010s: Memorials and wind

2011: BLPOA dedicated the Bass Lake Outlet Dam to Henry Frank Thiele, who passed away in February. A plaque is affixed on the dam in commemoration.

2012: Lake Winds Energy Park, a wind farm with fifty-six turbines visible to the north and east of Bass Lake, was built in Mason County.

2013: This year was Camp Morrison's hundredth anniversary. This campground is now Whispering Surf Campground at Bass Lake.

2020s: A new decade underway

2020: In June, Lake Michigan rose to its highest recorded level, causing the Bass Lake water level to remain high for more than a year.

2020–22: The COVID flu outbreak caused summer residents to stay longer at Bass Lake, and new folks arrived.

2025: Bass Lake Property Owners Association celebrates its 110th anniversary and documents over a century of Bass Lake history in the book *This Is Bass Lake: A Destination for Generations.*

Bass Lake Property Owners Association Officers

The leadership of the many people who served as officers in the Bass Lake Park Improvement Association / Bass Lake Property Owners Association is greatly appreciated. Their service through this all-volunteer, not-for-profit organization has been instrumental in sustaining the Bass Lake area for generations. (They were originally elected to one-year terms, and now they serve two-year terms.)

Please note: This list is from various historical sources and may not be 100 percent accurate. Any omissions are because officer names were not documented or were unknown.

Year	President	Vice President	Secretary	Treasurer
2024–25	Dan James	Russell Cross	Beth Walden	Elin Hartrum
2022–23	Wendy Jonkers	Dan James	Beth Walden	Dan James
2020–21	Wendy Jonkers	Dan Patsos	Judy Ringlein-Dunn	Fred Blase
2018–19	Kyle Chapman	Wendy Jonkers	Vicki Poplstein	Fred Blase
2016–17	Kyle Chapman	Wendy Jonkers	Vicki Poplstein	Barb Favre
2014–15	Chris Dunn	Kyle Chapman	Kyle Chapman	Barb Favre

Year	President	Vice President	Secretary	Treasurer
2012–13	Chris Dunn	Kyle Chapman	Kyle Chapman	Barb Favre
2010–11	Dennis McNeal	Chris Dunn	Kyle Chapman	Barb Favre
2008–09	Doug Osborn	Dennis McNeal	Kyle Chapman	Barb Favre
2006–07	Dick Ouweneel	Doug Osborn	Bill Cerny	Earl Woeltje
2004–05	Jim McKevitt	Lou Scarpino	Bill Cerny	Earl Woeltje
2002–03	Willard Mears	Lou Scarpino	Vacant	Ashley Gannett
2000–01	Russell Cross	Willard Mears	Sally Ouweneel / Sandra Cross	Ashley Gannett
1998–99	Everett Davidson	Russell Cross / Clarence Haus	Linda Osborn	Ashley Gannett
1996–97	John Gilbert	Clarence Haus	Joan Moranty	Ashley Gannett
1995	John Gilbert	Ronald Hamelen	Linda Sloughter	Ashley Gannett
1993–94	James Miller	Nancy Caruso	Linda Sloughter	Elizabeth Collins
1991–92	E.G. Stanley Baker	James Miller	Ashley Gannett	Elizabeth Collins
1989–90	Robert Scheuermann	Walter Richsteig	Ashley Gannett	Elizabeth Collins
1987–88	Eugene Becker	Robert Scheuermann	Ashley Gannett	Elizabeth Collins
1985–86	Richard Kraybill	Eugene Becker	Josephine Piel	Elizabeth Collins

Year	President	Vice President	Secretary	Treasurer
1983–84	Carl W. Piel	Paul Egbert	Imogene Hart	Elizabeth Collins
1981–82	Henry Thiele Jr.	Carl W. Piel	Juanita Jepson	Elizabeth Collins
1979–80	Keith Barrons	Henry Thiele	Juanita Jepson	Elizabeth Collins
1977–78	Larry Lewis	Keith Barrons	Juanita Jepson	Elizabeth Collins
1976	George Collins	Keith Barrons	Helen Baedke	Elizabeth Collins
1975	George Collins	Larry Lewis	Helen Baedke	Elizabeth Collins
1974	George Collins	Larry Lewis	Helen Baedke	Elizabeth Collins
1973	Karl H. Jepson	George Collins	Helen Baedke	Ila Church
1972	Karl H. Jepson	George Collins	Louisa Meyer	Ila Church
1971	Graham Lyday	Howard Hansen	Louisa Meyer	Ila Church
1970	Walter Shaw	Graham Lyday	Louisa Meyer	Ila Church
1969	Walter Shaw	Graham Lyday	Louisa Meyer	Beverly Fix
1968	Walter Shaw	Frank Blymyer	Anna Endicott	Beverly Fix
1967	Herbert Carstens			
1966	Herbert Carstens	Walter Shaw	Anna Endicott	Mrs. Ben Brown

Year	President	Vice President	Secretary	Treasurer
1965	Herbert Carstens			
1964	Herbert Carstens	Hollis Tate	Marie Hillman	Mrs. Keith Barrons
1963	Herbert Carstens	William Lustoff	Marie Hillman	Mrs. Keith Barrons
1962	Harry Lynch	Herbert Carstens	Mrs. Donald Heurlen	Florence Shepler
1961	Garth Warner	Harry Lynch	Mrs. G.B. Hebblewhite	Florence Shepler
1960	Garth Warner	Harry Lynch	Mrs. G.B. Hebblewhite	Florence Shepler
1959	Bernard Alfredson	Garth Warner	Caroline Plummer	Florence Shepler
1958	Bernard Alfredson	Garth Warner	Caroline Plummer	Florence Shepler
1957	Ted Chapman	Graham Lyday	Gladys McKevitt	Florence Shepler
1956	Ted Chapman	B.V. Alfredson	Mrs. C. I. Pecoy	Florence Shepler
1955	Mary J. Lambrix	Ted Chapman	Ruth Johnson	Mrs. Louis Rischar
1954	Mary J. Lambrix	C. Pecoy	Ruth Johnson	Mrs. Louis Rischar
1953	Louis Decker	Mary J. Lambrix	Mrs. W. R. Johnson	Mrs. Earl Ronneberg
1952	Louis Decker	Mary J. Lambrix	Mrs. W. R. Johnson	Mrs. Earl Ronneberg
1951	Louis Decker	Carl Carlson	Mrs. W. R. Johnson	Mrs. Earl Ronneberg

Year	President	Vice President	Secretary	Treasurer
1950	Chauncey Pecoy	Marie Hillman	Gladys McKevitt	Mrs. Earl Ronneberg
1949				
1948	Gustave Heurlin	Chauncey Pecoy	Vera Samuel	Minnie Decker
1947	Gustave Heurlin	Chauncey Pecoy	Vera Samuel	Minnie Decker
1946	Gustave Heurlin	Chauncey Pecoy	Vera Samuel	Lou Decker
1945	Charles Petefish	Gustave Heurlin	Mrs. Sidney March	Lou Decker
1944	Charles Petefish		Mrs. Sidney March	Mary Lambrix
1943	Irving H. Wanzer	Ashley Craig	Marie Hillman	Mary Lambrix
1942	Irving H. Wanzer	Ashley Craig	Marie Hillman	
1941	Ernest Jacobs	Irving H. Wanzer	Marie Hillman	Mrs. Sidney March
1940	Ernest Jacobs	Harry Hillman Jr.	Marie Hillman	Mrs. Sidney March
1939	A.M. Nelson	Harry Hillman Jr.	Marie Hillman	Mrs. Sidney March
1938	A.M. Nelson	Harry Hillman Jr.	Marie Hillman	Mrs. Proctor
1937	A.M. Nelson	Harry Hillman Jr.	Marie Hillman	Mrs. Proctor
1936	A.M. Nelson	Harry Hillman Jr.	Marie Hillman	Mrs. Proctor

Year	President	Vice President	Secretary	Treasurer
1935	A.M. Nelson	Harry Hillman Jr.	Marie Hillman	Mrs. Proctor
1934	A.S. Morrison	Harry Hillman Sr.	Marie Hillman	Susie Summers
1933	A.S. Morrison	Marie Hillman	Louella Haigh	Susie Summers
1932	A.S. Morrison		Louella Haigh	Susie Summers
1931	R.C. White	Mrs. N. Gilbert	Louella Haigh	George Wales
1930	R.C. White	Mrs. N. Gilbert	Louella Haigh	George Wales
1929	Henry Thiele	Mrs. N. Gilbert	Marie Hillman	Sam Noyer
1928	Henry Thiele	A.S. Morrison	Marie Hillman	Sam Noyer
1927	George Heritage	A.S. Morrison	Marie Hillman	Sam Noyer
1926	Fred Blase			
1925	Fred Blase	Sol Roderick	Marie Hillman	Thomas Schlick
1924	Fred Blase		Marie Hillman	
1923	Fred Blase		Marie Hillman	
1922	Fred Blase		Cora M. Collins	A.H. Conrad
1921				

Year	President	Vice President	Secretary	Treasurer
1920	N.D. Gilbert	Mr. Graf	Lena Broomell	Mr. S. Day
1919	N.D. Gilbert	William Yardley	Lena Broomell	Mr. S. Day
1918	A.H. Conrad			
1917	A.H. Conrad		Lena Broomell	
1916	A.H. Conrad	Edgar Chapman	Lena Broomell	Mr. Day
1915	A.H. Conrad	Edgar Chapman	Lena Broomell	L.H. Wayt

Acknowledgments

The achievement of this lived history of Bass Lake near Pentwater, Michigan, was no small task. Innumerable hours, days, and weeks were spent researching, compiling, writing, and documenting information. *This Is Bass Lake: A Destination for Generations* is a strong testament to more than a century of lives well-lived and fondly remembered. It marks the 110th anniversary of the Bass Lake Property Owners Association, established in 1915 and whose membership now represents more than 265 properties.

For decades, a complete telling of Bass Lake history was contemplated … started … set aside … restarted … repeat. To "remember the day," residents documented family memories, stories, and snapshots; collected historical facts; preserved newspaper clippings and brochures; and created scrapbooks—all good things. But it wasn't until the summer of 2021—as the Bass Lake community was reconnecting following the worldwide COVID pandemic—that the BLPOA said, "Let's do a history book!"

As the committee delved deeper into this history project, it became clear that the volume of material acquired to document more than a century of Bass Lake history exceeded what could be contained in the pages of this book. Now that this information has seen the light of day, we want it to be available and easily accessible for readers interested in more of the Bass Lake story. For this reason, supplemental photos and information will be available on the Bass Lake Property Owners Association website: www.basslakepentwater.org.

This endeavor was a multigenerational team effort. We gratefully acknowledge the contributions and cooperation of the following:

For the hours of work to bring this book to fruition, our Bass Lake History

Committee: Barbara Barrow Achenbaum, Carla Barrow, Kyle and Pam Chapman, Wendy Wanzer Jonkers, and Charity Gilbert Monroe.

For their trust and unwavering support of the History Committee, our 2024–25 BLPOA officers and directors: Dan James, Russ Cross, Elin Hartrum, Beth Walden, Wendy Jonkers, Hank Thiele, Joe Cada, and Dan Tebos.

For sharing historical documents and Bass Lake family memories, stories, and photos that charmingly brought to life the joys and trials of life on Bass Lake from the earliest times to today, we acknowledge the following families: Achenbaum, Allen, Allen-Doster, Baker, Barrow, Becker, Behr, Blase, Cerny, Challoner, Chapman, Chlebana, Cross, Danoff, Decker, Dooley, Doty, Drayer, Dunn, Finch, Fraker, Gannett, Gilbert, Gilbert, Guenther, Haigh, Hartrum, Hillman, Holmes, Johnson, Jonkers, Kimball, Kraybill, Krecko, Lattin, Ligon, Maike, March, McKevitt, Mink, Monroe, Ouweneel, Patsos, Payleitner, Plummer, Poplstein, Ramsey, Shiff, Siegel, Thiele, Thompson, Torp, Walden, Wanzer, Warner, Wlodarski, Woeltje, and Wright.

For photographs and visuals: Frederick Allen, Scott Barrow, Chapman Family, Halona Olive Gustin, Randy Holmes, Wendy Jonkers, Alice Kimball, Charity Monroe, Dick Ouweneel, Pentwater Historical Society, Ramsey Family, Thiele Family, Wanzer Family, Dick Warner, Willis Wright, and Greg Zimmerman.

For news accounts we were so thankful to find: *Ludington Daily News,* for the effort it has put forth over the decades to document life on our Bass Lake. Thanks also to the *Mason County Press, Oceana's Herald-Journal,* and the former *Pentwater News.*

For their commitment to preserving and sharing local history: The Mason County Historical Society, Oceana County Historical & Genealogical Society, and Pentwater Historical Society.

Lastly, we deeply apologize to anyone we inadvertently left off this list, and we apologize for any content in this labor of love that was not accurate or was not properly acknowledged.

Our hope is that you have been drawn in by the stories shared in this book. How lucky are those who know Bass Lake. Its history gives us a sense of place—like coming home to family and friends. For newcomers, Bass Lake and its everlasting enchantment await.

—Bass Lake History Committee 2021–25

Resources

Personal Narratives (unpublished)

Challoner, Kim. 2024. "The Mink-Poplstein-Challoner Family Story: 5 Generations at Bass Lake."

Chapman, Neva Julia Gilbert. c. 1950–'60s. "The Origin of Gilbert's Addition to Bass Lake Park."

Doty, Olga. 1974. "My Fondness for Bass Lake."

Endicott, Anna Chapman. c. 1960s. "I Remember."

Endicott, Anna Chapman. c. 1960s. "Stories of Early Days, as Told to Her Children."

Finch, Alice Butcher. 1987. "History of Long Ago Summers at Bass Lake."

Finch, George Britton. 1976. "Bass Lake Memories of 70 Years."

Finch, John P. 1997. "Notes on Bass Lake History."

Gannett, Ashley and Bob. 1999. "The Gilbert Bass Lake Collection."

Gilbert, Dr. Robert. Undated. "Bass Lake Memories."

Haigh, Louella. Undated. "Early Remembrances of Bass Lake."

Hillman, Harry III. Undated. "Bass Lake History."

Hillman, Marie. 1955. "My Bit of the History of Bass Lake."

Holmes, Randy. 2024. "Bass Lake History: Auld Lang Syne."

Lattin, Myrtle Race. Undated. "Activities Up at the Lake."

Ligon, Betty Gilbert. 1999. "Bass Lake Memories."

McKevitt, Gladys McMullin. 1974. "Bass Lake History."

Payleitner, Chris Torp. 2023. "Lookout Cottage, Thiele Road."

Ramsey, John E. 2019. "R.R. Ramsey Cottage History: 100 Years of Bass

Lake Tradition."

Shiff, Jay. 2024. "Bass Lake History."

Thiele, Mary. 2024. "Ice Fishing on Bass Lake."

Walden, Beth Handrock. 2024. "The SHaRP Renters."

Walden, Beth and Dave. 2024. "The Story of the Fieldstone Cottage."

Wlodarski, Debbie. 2024. "Stories from the Past."

Books

Monroe, Charity Gilbert. 1994. *George B. Finch, Raconteur, The Life and Times of George Britton Finch*. Self-published.

Schrumpf, Florence. 1965. *Pentwater, 1853–1942*. Self-published.

Yaple, Reginald. 2013. *1913 Camp Morrison—The First 100 Years, 2013 Whispering Surf Camping Resort*. Self-published.

Newspapers / Newsletters

Bass Lake Property Owners Association spring newsletters. 1973 and 1984.

Cabot, James. 1982 and 1990. "Bass Lake, Major Resort Area for Century." *Ludington Daily News*. Nov. 18, 1982 and June 30, 1990.

Goudschaal, Claudia Schlick. 2010. "Pentwater Memories." Pentwater Historical Society winter newsletter.

Jensen, James R. 2021. "Bass Lake Resorts." *Ludington Daily News*. Aug. 13, 2021.

Jensen, James R. 2024. "Martin Perkins: Bass Lake & Pentwater Connections." *Ludington Daily News*. July 28, 2024.

Jonkers, Wendy. 2021. "Welcome to Pentwater." *Pentwater This Week*. August 2021.

Kiessel, Jeff. 2015. "Wishing Well Reopening Welcomed." *Ludington Daily News*. May 5, 2015.

Klevorn, Patti. 2021. "Generations, Friends Gather for Thiele Dedication at Bass Lake." *Oceana's Herald-Journal*. Sept. 8, 2021.

Ludington Daily News. 1956. "For Billy and Bea, a Tall Pine." Dec. 2, 1956.

Ludington Daily News. 1974. "Propose X-Way Alternate." April 19, 1974.

Ludington Daily News. 1974. "Tornado Damages Bass Lake Area." Aug. 12, 1974.

Ludington Daily News. 1974. "County Agencies OK Freeway's Location."
Oct. 1, 1974.

Ludington Daily News. 1986. "The Days the Rain Came." Sept. 18, 1986.

Pentwater Historical Society winter newsletter. 2008. "Pentwater Filling
Stations, Part II."

Pentwater News. 1932. "Lyman H. Wayt Victim of Ice at Bass Lake."
Feb. 26, 1932.

Pentwater News. 1947. "Mrs. Helen Wayt Laid to Last Rest." August 1947.

Petersen, Dave. 2008. "I Remember Bass Lake: A Conversation with
94-year-old Landowner Henry Thiele." *Ludington Daily News*.
Aug. 2, 2008.

Peterson, Paul. 1998. "100 Years and Bortell's Fisheries is Still Going
Strong." *Ludington Daily News*. June 26, 1998.

Scarbrough, Allison. 2015. "A Wish Granted." *Mason County Press*.
Apr. 1, 2015.

Historical Societies

Oceana County Historical & Genealogical Society, www.oceanahistory.
org.

Pentwater Historical Society, www.pentwaterhistoricalsociety.org.

The Mason County Historical Society, www.masoncountymihistory.org.

Miscellaneous (minutes, leaflets, letters, websites)

Bass Lake Park Improvement Association minutes (various).

Bass Lake Property Owners Association minutes (various).

Bass Lake Recreation Park By-Laws and Rules. 1886.

Leaflet: Camp Morrison.

Leaflet: Smert's Resort. c. 1973.

Leaflet: Thiele Real Estate.

Leaflet: Wayt's Hotel. c. early 1900s.

Letter from Alice Butcher Finch to her family at Christmas. 1987.

Letter from Bass Lake Property Owners Association to US Treasury
Department regarding tax-exempt status and name change. July 24,
1969.

Letter from Bass Lake Property Owners Association President

L. Graham Lyday regarding highway corridor choices for US Hwy 31 near Bass Lake. c. 1971.

Letter from George B. Finch to Mrs. Mary Lambrix. 1954.

Letters from Clara Parbs to Bass Lake Park Improvement Association regarding aftermath of November 1940 Armistice Day Storm. November 17 and 18, 1940.

"Bortell's Fisheries: 125+ Years of Fried, Smoked and Fresh Fish," www.lakeshorevacationer.com.

Consumers Energy, www.consumersenergy.com.

Ferwerda's Bass Lake Resort, www.basslakeresortmi.com.

Pentwater Building Stories, www.pentwaterbuildingstories.com/ptw-train.

West Michigan Pike, www.michiganbeachtowns.com.

Whispering Surf Campground at Bass Lake, www.whisperingsurfcampground.com.

About the Authors

The Bass Lake History Committee's six members are connected in unique ways yet share a common heritage—two are sisters, two are married, and two are third cousins. Collectively, they represent more than 500 years of family history at west Michigan's Bass Lake.

Barbara Barrow Achenbaum lives in Connecticut but is happiest at Franklin's Folly, her grandfather's cottage purchased seventy-five years ago. Her professional experience includes brand management, communications, and grant writing. She now helps preserve stories of family and friends for future generations.

Carla Barrow resides in Illinois. Her lifelong passion for Bass Lake made her a logical fit for this history project. As a teenager, she developed an interest in storytelling through interviews and photography. Today, she's a self-taught archivist preserving memorabilia through scrapbooks she gifts to volunteer organizations.

Kyle and Pam Chapman live in Indiana and spend retirement summers at Bass Lake. Kyle's family history goes back to 1896 and his great-grandfather Gilbert's Bass Lake vision. A past president of the Bass Lake Property Owners Association, Kyle currently leads the Bass Lake Improvement Board. Pam has a communications background and now pursues her interest in genealogy and historical preservation.

Wendy Wanzer Jonkers resides in North Carolina and is a fourth generation Bass Laker. Growing up, she loved hearing stories of her parents' childhood Bass Lake summers. As president of the Bass Lake Property Owners Association in 2021, she cast the vision of preserving and sharing more than a century of stories.

Charity Gilbert Monroe lives in Illinois and vacations at the cottage built by her great-grandmother. Charity's family has enjoyed Bass Lake sailing and boating since 1902. A retired engineer and avid photographer, she's self-published three books of family history.